Rest Your
Weary Mind

Rest Your
Weary Mind:

Humorously Rewriting the
Narrative From Within

ABIGAIL RENOLA TJADEN

PUNCHLINE
PUBLISHERS

First paperback edition November 2023

Cover design by Chelsea Scott

Illustrations copyright © 2023 by Abigail Renola Tjaden

ISBN 978-1-955051-22-4

Published by Punchline Publishers

www.punchlineagency.com

www.artjaden.com

@artjadendesigns

To my mom Vicki, grandmother Renola, and Elaine

*I wouldn't be the woman I am without you.
Thank you for loving me and raising me to be
fiercely independent, ready to go out into this
big beautiful world to pursue my dreams.*

Contents

ahshit

Foreword
by Bonnie Weeks

I t was the toilet.

    If someone was going to be bold enough to draw a picture of a toilet and put it on a greeting card saying "ah shit" and rest it front-and-center at a women's conference about being authentic, then I was instantly sold.

There's nothing more authentic than every single one of us sitting on the throne. People usually buy a card to share it, but after four years, I'm still hoarding this one.

As someone who's re-storied myself many times through faith transition, divorce, parenting, sex, nude photography, poetry, business owning and what it means to be a woman, I so appreciate Abigail's humor and honesty.

My work as a coach, teacher, podcast host and writer allows me the opportunity to work with many different people.

Everyone wants to be unapologetic.

No one wants to feel small.

There's a different journey for each of us to name what we want and embrace the skin we're in.

The cool part is that we don't grow alone. It's books like this that remind us that we're in it together.

As someone who is walking the path and brave enough to share about the process, Abigail doesn't shy away from saying anything.

The way she shares her personal stories, space for reflection and some of the practices that continue to bring her home to herself, we get to add to our own self-care toolkit.

Be it stress baking, buying yourself beautiful things "just because" or giving yourself permission to actually just enjoy the damn thing, this book feels like a friend who fist bumps you after your three-day constipation comes to an end.

We're here for the real shit.

INTRODUCTION:

All Starts Here

I n Portland, Oregon, the weather can't make up its mind. The rain is falling one minute and then, like a flip of a switch, the sun shines through. The phrase here is "wait five minutes" and it couldn't be more true. This cool, wet precipitation followed by the warmth sharing some Vitamin D can send anyone into a "what am I even supposed to wear" panic. One minute Portlanders are dodging quickly from place to place taking cover from the rain, and the next minute resting like cats, extending limbs, basking in the sunshine. These Pacific Northwest weather patterns are similar to my daily anxious thoughts.

I don't know about you, but most days I toggle back and forth between self-doubt and self-confidence. I go from feeling a bit down to feeling on fire; ready to crawl back in bed only minutes later to move mountains. The difference comes when I choose to push past my initial mental clamor and step into a space of calm renaissance that says *I've got this*. I lean into that still small voice which reminds me to seize the day. There is a hope that rests in my heart, guiding me to believe that I was created for so much goodness.

This book is my attempt at sharing some

personal stories and reflections on how I have worked through negative self-talk, anxious thoughts, and self-doubt. Here, I offer guidance on taming those spiraling thoughts and shifting your mindset. You may find yourself saying "oh I have gone through this too" as you read and relate to these short vignettes matched with visual components designed by me. I want to encourage you to take a deep inhale and exhale out a sigh of relief. Someone else has experienced something similar. You can rest your weary mind from the worry and anxiety that you face each day.

Life has a way of throwing us curve balls and challenges around every corner. Some seasons feel especially heavy. I want to help you step out of those anxious thought patterns. I want to help you throw them down to the curb and rest on my shoulders as I share my own experiences and growth. I have seen growth in how I handle stress thrown at me. Where once I would spiral, now I am able to take a pause and breathe, letting go of what is out of my control. I have learned how to lean into my emotions, even those big feels, and give validation to them. I don't need to stuff them down or seek others' approval. I'm not saying I'm perfect or without these moments of self-doubt, but I have walked in and out of joy-filled times.

As a part of our journey together, I want you to write in this book. Yes! You read me correctly. There are going to be prompts and activities for you to journal throughout to help you reflect on your own experiences. Grab a pen and jot down notes in the margins and in the provided pages. Take out some markers or colored pencils and color in the illustrations. The quote pages in each chapter are meant for you to rip out (or neatly cut out) to place at your workstation, bedroom wall, or bathroom mirror.

With many stressful moments and times in our lives, we can handle what life throws our way.

I hope you can further explore what it means to let your mind rest, let go of all the things that are out of your control, and find freedom from the inner critic and nagging thought patterns. Like the Portland weather that no one can completely prepare for, there's an art of learning to release yourself to the elements. We have to find a way to do this in our day-to-day lives, rain or shine.

Be gentle with yourself. You got this.

Blind Date:
Meet Bertolli

I recently went on a blind date. As I got ready that morning, flying around my apartment, trying to stay busy to distract myself, my mind got busier. Cue the party beginning in my stomach. Both excitement and nervousness knit together in a huge ball, and my gut was starting to unravel quickly. This mixture of the unknown and meeting someone new made my insides want to be on the outside.

With all the online profiles and apps, is it possible to go out with someone I've never seen? Someone my friend Elizabeth, and not an algorithm, had picked? Someone named Derek? Are her matchmaking skills better than undercover coding? Better than my creative eye? How will I know who I am going on a date with when I don't even know his height or hair color? What if there is so much awkward silence? What if the only thing we have in common is that we both like ketchup? Wouldn't this be easier blindfolded?

If you can't tell already, my nerves were through the roof. Going on dates in general is not something I have done with any frequency. Rarely in my 30s have I gotten asked out, and it was even more rare to be set up. In my golden college years, I was colliding with guys naturally in classes or at events. Being in close proximity with young men was fun, thrilling, and easy. It was my effortless era, having a flirty personality and genuine smile helped me win guys over. Of course in my 20s I had my whole life ahead of me, so it was fine to keep it casual. This dating scene a decade later seemed like unfamiliar new territory. I didn't want to put pressure on myself that "he could be the one," but it was hard not to be hopeful in meeting someone new.

I took a shower, worked on my hair, and started putting "my face on." I wanted to present myself in the best way, but still felt, like always, the effort would be wasted. Some anxious thoughts started to rise up because I felt a pressure on myself to look good to impress this guy. Was this guy making sure he put his daily moisturizer on with sunscreen? Did he take time to pluck out stray eyebrow hairs? I reached for my mascara. Raising the wand too quickly, I stabbed my eye with the brush end. Shit! Black chunks floated around my contact and I touched a finger to my eye. Got it with one swoop. A tear started to well up and I quickly reached for a tissue. My hand was shaking the whole time, causing tension in my shoulders. I tried to blink away the irritation. Blind date? I couldn't see a thing! In these moments the expectation of what I wanted to happen—this guy to find me attractive—and what was actually happening—nervousness that gave me a chunky black eye—all collided to cause me to doubt my worth.

I fixed the makeup, but I started to get flushed under my face cream. My cheeks, along with my whole body, were having a hard time regulating their temperature. I needed fresh air. I threw open a window in the living room. Before I knew it, my usually bad stomach got so bad that I had to lie down on my floor. I rubbed my abdomen and focused on my breathing. My nerves were taking over. Unrealistic expectations were finding their way to my heart. I didn't need to focus on the big questions, but I was—like, were our values going to align, could I trust him and feel safe with him, would this thing go so far that he would meet my family? ALL the ramblings were running wild in my head. I had to calm the eff down. Without warning, my mind had taken over my body and emotions in unexpected ways, seemingly beyond my control. If I fixated too much on all of the unknowns, my body got so stressed. Deep inside I was truly struggling with feeling embarrassed about my age, not having more dating experience, and setting myself up for another rejection.

After lying down on the ground, I decided movement might keep my mind off of the date. I danced in my living room to Lizzo songs and Chance the Rapper lyrics. The anxiety would rise here and there, but I spoke calmly, telling myself to chill. I wanted to stand in confidence and not in the fear of the unknowns.

But blind dates are not a chill situation! Everything inside me tried to predict what he would look like, who he could be, and why my friend thought this setup would be good. I felt like I was supposed to be good at this dating thing. So many of my girl-friends went on multiple dates each week, each with different guys. It was actually considered normal to do so. Was there time for me to jump into the game and flex my get-to-know-you chops? Did I have what it takes to make a good first impression so he would want to go out again? No matter how hard I tried I could not stop the comparison game inside of me. I truly wanted to be good at this dating world, even though I had no experience in blind dates. Now I was accidentally stabbing my eye over nerves due to poten-tially letting down a stranger?

10:30 a.m. and still two hours 'til the lunch date. Some peo-ple hold stress in their shoulders, back, or neck. My stress goes straight to my stomach due to how I perceive the risks before me. These rumblings in my lower abdomen seem to rise up when I give agency to my negative voice. Almost like a fight or flight switch gets turned on. Maybe some homemade sourdough cinnamon rolls would help. I used the internet to look up the recipe, and set my computer off to the side on a surface I'd wiped free of crumbs. Prepping the area where I was working with flour, I was ready to roll out the dough. As I scrolled through the recipe, fingers covered in white dust, I learned that olive oil was required to handle the dough. I got out my full bottle of Bertolli brand extra virgin oil.

I finished making the dough and began rolling out the rolls. Vigorously sprinkling flour across my counter, I grabbed the dough and plopped it down. Reaching for my wooden rolling pin, I started working the dough down, flipping it after two passes on the top. I moved my body from one side of the counter to the other, back and forth, with more pep in my step than the last. I knew I was in a time crunch, so I started letting the rolling pin rip. The pressure was strong, intentional was my grip, and fast were my rotations of the tool. Just a few more passes. Gotta get this done. Go faster now. Spin that rolling pin and add more oomph. Go.. Go.. BOOM… I must have been getting wild with my rolling pin, because before I realized what happened, I full-on knocked the olive oil bottle over onto my laptop keyboard. Unfortunately, I don't have kids, and have not perfected the "motherly reflex." I

bolted my arm out, quickly grabbing the fallen bottle, but more than a cup of liquid had already begun seeping into every crevice of the keyboard. The keys were slimy and shimmering with Bertolli olive oil. I frantically dashed for paper towels to soak up the oil, and did a super quick google search on my phone: "how to clean up oil spill on laptop."

"Socks," the collective *they* agreed. Place a sock on the end of the vacuum cleaner hose, and suck away. So there I was, in my bra, jumping over to the closet to pull out my vacuum and grab a sock. I did five passes over the keys, but still had a blind date to get ready for.

The cinnamon rolls still had yet to go into the oven. Leaving them half-finished on the counter, I was more concerned about my computer. I laid some paper towel sheets on the keys and shut the screen down, laying it upside down. (Another hot tip from the internet.) I was in a time crunch, people! I was still half-dressed and needed to find a top to wear. On the move. Gone.

After I found an outfit to wear, I went back to spread the butter, cinnamon, and cardamom ingredients across the dough. With gentle fingers, I stretched and rolled the gooey sourdough into a long log shape. Cutting sections with a knife, I placed each section into the pan. The whole time, I couldn't make eye contact with my laptop. I didn't have time to be sad. I needed to pull myself together for this meetup. In an attempt to shift my mind from the stress of putting myself out there, that I might fail at this dating thing, I definitely felt like a failure in trying to make these rolls. What a disaster my kitchen was, and now I had a laptop upside down with olive oil dripping down. I wanted to cancel this date, stat. But I didn't want to be someone who "ghosts," or somebody who doesn't follow through.

Leaving my house I made it to the local coffee shop. With my curly hair, tight jeans, and white top I rested against a brick wall on Belmont street, as if I was waiting for Top Gun Tom Cruise to arrive. My mystery date was running late. I waited, waited, and waited some more. He came around the corner and was in no hurry. He was tall, buzzed head, and smiled with a big ol' goober grin on his face. Instantly my nerves left my body, and after chatting for two minutes I knew this was not a love match. I just was not attracted to him.

Because I know some of you might care more about my computer than the actual date, my computer was a bit of a hot mess. I didn't get to check on it until after the date ended. The whole time I was away, I was quietly concerned but never mentioned this debacle to my date. When I returned home I flung open my front door, launched myself up a flight of stairs, and rounded the corner to the kitchen. The keyboard was STICKY. The oil was not just confined to the keys: the screen was now tacky to the touch and had a lightning bolt running from left to right, like a good David Bowie face paint. The screen technically still worked but it was going to be annoying to have to look beyond the bubbly dysfunction to design my next art project. I looked on my phone for when the Apple store had open hours. Crossing my fingers, I hoped at least someone there could help me.

My computer works fine now, just fine enough. And the rolls were awesome. They worked out after all; all was not lost! I baked them the second I got home from the date with Derek, waiting 10 minutes of preheat time and 22 minutes of 400 degrees baking time 'til I could devour them. The flavors of cinnamon, warm cardamom, ginger, and nutmeg all swirled together with every bite. I ate two rolls while I sat on my living room floor and processed my mess of a day.

But before you stop to go make yourself some delicious homemade cinnamon rolls, we gotta clean up our thoughts around preparing for a date.

My nerves and expectations got the best of me.

Preparing sourdough while applying makeup for that date with Derek revealed my heart: just like the oil seeping into my computer, my anxious thoughts were taking over and spilling into my chest. I was distracted and allowed myself to dwell on ideas around this guy before I even met him. I had to choose a way to slow my system down, to focus on what I could control, and let go of everything that was out of my hands. I made cinnamon rolls. They nearly became the most expensive cinnamon rolls of my life because they almost cost me a whole new computer. In the end, they were too sticky and just needed more time to rise. I wish I could have given myself more time in every aspect of this baking process. It was a last-minute decision to distract myself by baking something at all. I needed to keep my hands busy. I just had too much nervousness around meeting a guy for the first time.

I should state the date went okay. We got our chai teas—neither of us being coffee drinkers (see, we did have something in common!)—and took a few loops around Laurelhurst Park. But the pressure my body went through preparing for that chai and walk through the park—it came from somewhere.

I know what that "somewhere" is now—I wanted this stranger to like me for how I looked on the outside, but still wanted him to get to know me with all my imperfections and quirks. This was important to me because I wanted to be seen and known for who I am. I was putting unnecessary pressure on myself, caring too much about how he would perceive me. Ironically, the whole time we were together, I hid my silly ways out of nervousness. I definitely didn't tell him about Bertolli meeting my keyboard.

Talking with my girlfriends, there seems to be a universal sentiment that we are expected to be our best selves, never showing a flaw, especially when making first impressions. No matter what, we are to be confident, know what we want (but not too much), and go after it (but don't come on too strong). As women we are pressured to show up excited and happy that someone wants to get to know us, no matter what. It is on the guys' terms, allowing them to have agency first, if they like us, if they find us attractive.

Instead, the narrative needed to switch inside of me. I was able to discern if I wanted to get to know him. I was able to decide if he was worthy of my time and energy. All too often I find myself in a cycle of *why doesn't he like me*, but maybe it is for me to stand on my own two feet and be confident that I know what I need and desire. He might not be for me, and I might not be for him, and either way, I still have worth just because I am me.

At the same time, right alongside a universal push to be my best was my responsibility to acknowledge the pressure and expectations I had put on myself. I was the one with the stomach ache, the slick keys, and the mascara eyeball. I was the one who needed to challenge my inner narrative that told me I would somehow mess things up, say the wrong thing, and be too much. I had convinced myself that there was something wrong with me. I know now that this comes from a deep insecurity that I will never be truly known by a partner or one day spouse. I fear my sensitive heart, my deep feelings, and tendency to cry easily will overwhelm someone. That I'll be too much.

TOO MUCH? Really.

TOO MUCH for a guy who was kind but wasn't able to hold the conversation? Who worried about getting his white sneakers muddy? In Portland? If I give him an ounce of credit, maybe he had a wall up and didn't know how to open up and be vulnerable. Maybe he was working through his own insecurities and feels rejection often. Maybe he poked his own eye while plucking stray brow hairs?

We focus on the wrong stuff.

I wish I had chosen to focus that morning on showing up for myself, on seeing myself in new situations in a positive light, instead of questioning everything that was out of my control. I believed that my self-worth and validation came from within, but I needed to drop the internal mind games. I had hoped White Sneakers Boy could be the next best person in my world. I spent hours prepping and baking and Macgyvering my way through every possibility before even meeting him. I could have saved my energy and placed it in enjoying a cup of tea while reading a book or journaling. Or even just learning a new song on guitar, not stressing over something I had no control over.

A bit of nervousness is a good sign. It means we're excited about what may take shape. I believe that the perfect blind date might be out there. But I know nothing can transpire unless we breathe.

Breathe in the present. For me, it smells like cinnamon.

WE FOCUS ON THE WRONG STUFF

Turn on YOUR FAVORITE 𝄞 SONG AND DANCE AROUND

CHECK IN ON YOURSELF

Fill in this page and take a look at what you need to let go of. Find a new song that gets your feet moving, and dance around in your living room. Be sure to turn it up a little; let your neighbors guess what you are up to.

CHAPTER 2

Training Uptown

When you are meeting friends for dinner at 7:00 p.m. in New York City, every second counts. There are a million things that can go wrong when catching a subway train, and one day they all did.

6:19 p.m.

I am enjoying a beautiful day in NYC, walking around, exploring some brownstone streets.

6:20 p.m.

I have been finding my way around the city just fine over the past week, taking trains everywhere. I am in NYC on vacation to stay with a few friends and explore the city. My main goals are to spend time in Brooklyn, see as much art as I can in Manhattan, draw a bunch of the architecture and food, and take the ferry out to Staten Island. There is no schedule, but I want to hop from train to train, experiencing as much as I can.

Must meet up with Anna and Russell for dinner. Even after a long day of navigating various Brooklyn boroughs, I have enough energy to socialize. I need to eat sometime. I know it is going to take me at least 45 minutes to get to my destination. I decide I need to give myself a little extra time to make sure that I can meet up with my friends for dinner on time. Drilled in my head from my youth, it was important to follow through with commitments and to show respect to those I was meeting. It was crucial to be there when agreed upon.

6:21 p.m.

Glance at my phone and notice the time. I needed to leave five minutes ago!!! SHIT!

Whole body, full throttle, feet to the ground, all out...NOW RUSHING!

6:25 p.m.

Running or walking fast is the only option. Get to the train station. Scan my subway card. Loud beep noise as my thighs ram into the turnstyle. Flip the dumb thing around and scan it correctly this time. Then I WAIT and wait some more. I quickly walk down the steps, but I'm on the wrong platform, so I hit the stairs again to walk back up and around to go the other direction. Passing by some musicians, the tote-bagged hipsters, and a mom with a stroller, kids in tow. No stress, no worries. *I got this.* I hate when this happens. I immediately feel stupid from my miscalculation and being disoriented. I notice a dialogue starting to take shape in the back of my mind. *Quiet down! This stuff happens all the time. Don't feel embarrassed about it.*

6:31 p.m.

I look down at my phone and search the platform for the train signs. Find the color, the letter, the direction of the one I want to board. Any chance the next train I need is coming? Rumblings from the other direction. The ground shakes and rattles. How do we know it is structurally safe to be so far underground? Trying not to look frazzled, I take a breath to remind myself I am going to make it to my friends. I relax my shoulders but grip my backpack straps tighter. I give off a strong *I am from here* vibe and a kind twenty-something gal asks me how to get to her destination. I don't have time to really listen. Inside I am flattered, but I just give a small smile. Moving on and away I go. Earlier in the week I moved with ease on the subway, but this felt so different. I sensed the clock was ticking away. *Tick. Tick. Tick.*

6:35 p.m.

My thoughts quickly spiral and the sweat starts to move down my back. Does anybody know North, South, East, and/or West underground? Those living in NYC surely get familiar quickly with how to get to Queens over Manhattan or Brooklyn. But sometimes, the sign just says, "Downtown" or "Uptown." Every city has its own downtown and uptown, but being in the depths of the earth, below all the traffic lights and taxi cars, it just feels different. I get turned around more easily underground as my phone goes in and out of service. Relying on Google Maps may not be the best idea. I don't like this feeling that I messed up or that I'm ruining some dinner reservations. Will the table even still be available when I get there?

6:37 p.m.

Where is that train I need? I start to pace the platform, never stepping over the yellow line. Don't want to get too close. Stay away from the ledge, stay away from the people, and keep calm. Checking the time to my final destination, sweat starts to form on my hands. WOW. There it is, the nervous system is saying hello. Wiping them on my thighs, I notice the digital signs above my head flash new train numbers and arrival times. *Hello, summer if you could just be kind to me. I don't need a sweat attack ALL over my body. Oh wait, I am not being kind to me.*

6:38 p.m.

We are the rats, running through a maze, trying to find the best spot to eat, rest, repeat.

With WiFi on the rails, there is no need for an actual paper map. Glancing at my phone, which I am holding with a death grip, I make sure I am on the path toward the restaurant. I know I looked just a minute ago, but it comforts me to keep looking over and over. I don't like when I am not able to figure this stuff out on the first try. I feel ashamed that as a grown adult I am messing plans up for others. *You were doing fine all week, relying on digital maps and your directionally-challenged intuition. But there was never a timetable.* Woof. My stomach starts to churn, from the stress and being genuinely super hungry.

6:39 p.m.

I just want to get to my friends. Repeat the phrase another twenty-five times. If I say it slower it will make me feel better. But it doesn't. When I needed to "see" where I was going back in the early 2000s, I had my Garmin close by. Going in the wrong direction was signaled by taking a path that wasn't green or illuminated. Don't tell anyone but sometimes I would hold the whole darn thing in my right hand when the suction on the dashboard gave out. I wish I could hold the train route in my hands, to see if I was moving towards my final destination. *You can't do this on your own. You aren't capable. There is something wrong with you.*

6:40 p.m.

The WiFi works for the most part as I wait, but my phone is on the fritz and the battery is about to die. Do I have the correct restaurant mapped out? I text Anna that I would likely be late. No response. I see the "..." text bubble appear for a second and then it disappears. Are my messages even going through? I forgot to bring my personal charger. Why do I have the cord, but not the charging device? A wave of stress takes over my body. Growing up my dad always said that if I was late to anything, it was unacceptable. To be on time then was actually to be fifteen minutes early. Thanks, Dad, for the advice. Not helping right now. Where the heck is that train?

6:42 p.m.

FINALLY. Boarding the train and it is packed. We are sardines, smelling so fresh on this warm summer evening. Looking down at my phone, still no reply from Anna. But everything is going to work out from here. I make it in the direction I need to go. Business attire, book lovers, grocery store bags, and cellphone social media scrollers are all together. We are going to make it to our final location. I will be late but there is nothing I can do now. *Nothing is wrong now. You can do this.*

6:46 p.m.

A conductor gets on the overhead intercom and informs us that this train is going to stop and will not be continuing service due to construction ahead. *WHAT!!!!!!!*

CONSTRUCTION. Of course, there is always something happening, workers doing their thing, especially in the city that never sleeps.

The goal was to see Anna and Russell for dinner, and now I have no idea how that is going to happen. These are the salt of the earth couple who really listen. They just moved to New York City, and gave an open invitation to visit. I am that friend who takes people up on their offers. I never feel like a third wheel with them. *It is official, I was going to be wasting their time.* Waves of guilt and selfishness spill over and through my body.

6:48 p.m.

My plans are literally getting derailed. As my body temperature starts to rise, I take a deep breath of stale subway air and exit the train. The doors fling wide open and I leap into the great unknown. Standing on the platform, I don't know which direction to go. Holding my phone in my hands, I retype in the address to the restaurant, hoping it will be smart enough to redirect me. Do I need to go up and out or up and over? Am I going to miss the next train? In my head, I am dodging the anxious conversation playing out: *You are going to be so late. Anna and Russell told you a specific time and now you are going to waste their time. Being late is unacceptable.* The expectations I had over the whole situation are completely unreasonable. The inner dialogue continues. *Did I not have the correct app on my phone to have known this wasn't going to happen? How did I not see this coming?*

6:50 p.m.

Here we go. I got this. I really hope I got this. I go up the stairs, back around to only go back down to catch a train going in the opposite direction for just two stops. Constantly consulting my phone feels better than having a meltdown with a stranger asking for help. I get really turned around. The GPS on my phone can't keep up with my new location, and the WiFi is not connecting properly. More anxiety starts to rise. The graffiti billboards and dingy white tiles are not comforting. The tunnels all start to look the same. The fast pace of commuters during rush hour makes my nervousness rise. I'm really not good at navigating underground. I think if you live in NYC and you are a frequent subway rider, you just get accustomed to these setbacks. People have to exit trains and find new routes all the time. But I am a Portlander on vacation, who navigates best above ground. My easy breezy West Coast vibe is not colliding well with this regimented, punctual transit system tonight. Walking everywhere in Portland, where streets are organized alphabetically and numerically, makes this new system of knowing the final destination for the trains nearly impossible. Because everything in NYC is so expensive, saving money by using public transit seems like the wise choice to make, but now I am feeling like a rat running all over the place.

7:24 p.m.

   With train delays, and more construction detours, I have to exit one station to walk over to another. As I rush to the exit area, I come upon the turnstiles. Oh my goodness, how I don't want to look like a fool trying to get through. Working professionals in blue suits, moms pushing strollers, hundreds of tourists—we're all being funneled through one section of the station. What genius decided that these metal contraptions were the best option? Jabbing my hand down my shorts pocket, I locate the coveted metro card. I scan my card upside down. BEEP!!! An error message appears. I turn my card around and try swiping again. BEEP!!! The green light unlocks the metal arms so I can push myself forward. I would like to tell you I pretend I am a football linebacker and charge ahead, and leave everyone to dust in my wake. But there is only one turnstile and it is the standing tall variety. I get stuck— like halfway in between the arms that spin and the ones that don't. Moving so quickly and with force, trying to be confident in the "I totally know what I am doing" mentality, I end up slamming my body into the metal arms on the right. Full-on BAM into the metal, for sure leaving a bruise by tomorrow. I wince and try to shake off the pain in my hip. I squeeze my way to the other side, but not without embarrassment written all over my face. The sweat is running down my back and I can't believe I am still beneath street level.

7:30 p.m.

People push past me as I tap at my phone, searching for a way out. Google Maps is not helping as I get sideswiped by a large backpack. Flashing signs overhead give more train arrival times. *Did I already pass these shredded billboards with graffiti?* Crowds of people moving, criss-crossing, and weaving through street performers set up on the platform. I try to locate some stairs that will lead me out of this maze. *Not my luck today. Not doing well. So exhausted.*

8:05 p.m.

My phone cuts in and out, with no service, and then service again.

At this point, I am well over an hour late for dinner. I feel my blood pressure rising. I feel the stress increasing every time my phone cuts in and out. Being turned around is losing its romantic luster.

On the show *Who Wants to be a Millionaire?*, contestants can phone a friend and ask their advice for one of their questions. Underground with my phone at 1%, I have one chance left to get this right. I call Anna. I am so relieved to hear her voice. She doesn't seem bothered that I am running late and has a few suggestions on what route I can take next. Despite her soothing, I am still super overwhelmed and my body lets another round of sweat run down my back. *I am swimming in sweat and a sea of strangers.*

There seems to be so many times specifically while riding the New York City subway when every minute counts, every second is accounted for. You are always rush-rush-rushing, but then, you're forced to be wait-wait-waiting. People fall asleep while train riding, and people are confidently reading, consuming music through headphones, or playing the latest game of Candy Crush on their phones. New Yorkers have perfected this ease of rushing to resting. A complete contrast of jumping aboard a subway car to being lulled to sleep the next minute. Bodies with standing room only crammed together more than sardines in a tin.

Everyone is at the mercy of the public transit system, moving you from underground to walking long blocks filled with buildings scraping the sky. Each New Yorker is used to this transfer of time and space. I, on the other hand, am not.

8:15 p.m.

I arrive and my friend Anna throws her arms around me. I finally make it right where I need to be. The drama of the hour before quickly slips away as I pull up a wooden chair to the tightly packed table setting, dimly lit by candles. We eat and drink together, enjoying the meal and evening. I reach for my wine glass with my right hand and I give the wine a swish. As I take another sip, I release the day's stress, knowing that tomorrow is going to be a new day. Crossing my fingers, I know I can get anywhere I want to go, it just might take me an extra hour.

CHECK IN ON YOURSELF

Make a list of 10 realities that worry you and then list 10 friends who have dealt with something similar. Let this be a fun exercise to remind you that this stuff happens to everyone.

YOU ARE
RIGHT
WHERE
YOU NEED TO
BE

CHAPTER 3

Downpour on the High Line

Blistered feet, my new black high-top Vans squished and pounded the ground beneath them. It was August 2019, and I was in New York City for a tradeshow. Setting up at the Javits Center for The National Stationery Show, I showcased my greeting card collection to potential buyers under the brightest fluorescent lights known to planet earth. One evening after a long day of chit-chatting with what seemed like hundreds of people, I thought it would be fun to revisit a favorite spot nearby, the High Line. The weather seemed fine, but I didn't check my phone for an actual weather reading. I didn't have a clue that the Manhattan sky was about to burst open with a heavy downpour.

The High Line is a historical elevated rail line found within the meatpacking district in Chelsea, Manhattan that offers a unique perspective of New York City. This public park shares a distinctive connection between what are public and private spaces. Winding paths are filled with wildflowers, grasses, and huge metal pieces of art. Through the thicket of shrubs you could take in the skyscrapers, colorful murals, and people smoking cigarettes off their balconies. Colorful flags hang from interior windows letting the world know what the inhabitants believed in. This old rail line was redesigned with wooden deckchair benches that can roll and slide together. It is a place full of intimate spots that encourage you to linger, rest, and open a book. With elements from post-industrial infrastructure, the now transformed green spaces make it feel like you are walking on history.

My feet hit metal stairs. One, two, three steep steps, up, up, up. Then steps four, five, six up more steep stairs. Up up up I continued to go. Seven, eight, nine, my feet kept rising as my calves started burning. Ten, eleven, twelve, are we there yet? Thirteen, fourteen…twenty…and finally I was higher than one story. This seemingly secret stairway found outside at the base of the Chelsea Market, only recognizable by a small sign posted ahead, was leading me towards the sky. Walking on wooden boards, I rounded the corner and saw the direction I wanted to go. Ahead was an alleyway that opened up into an urban secret garden. These express passageways rise above the modern streets. Here, lifted high, I didn't have to compete with the cars or traffic. I was a part of the tourist flow of foot traffic, and I was on a mission. I had to get to my favorite spot—the place near the other end of the one mile long passage with wooden high-rise benches, a part where the artist Piet Olduf framed the street view.

From the High Line, the view was different. I was able to see in, look through, and almost physically be with the people in their apartments, condos, and spaces. My outdoor space was adjacent to their kitchen or bedroom. I had dreamt of returning to this passageway, to sit back on the wooden tall bench, and stare into the street. My first time visiting the High Line was with an architect friend who showed me that special spot, where my eyes saw everything with a new and fresh perspective. It was thrilling to be so high up from the ground, looking out at the world and my surroundings.

I had to get back to that spot. No matter what. See, there was this pause in all the commotion around me when I sat there. It was as if observing others rush around brought a sense of calm into my body. I liked how an actual wooden frame gave the street at this spot a contextual vantage point. It seemed like anything coming in or out of the frame was being captured in real time, as if you were watching an edited film. There was a chance for myself to relive a special connection I had with this friend. He told me about how the artist wanted us to sit, reflect, take in the sights, but to rest. I reminisced about our whole conversation around philosophical ideas about taking up space, and our thoughts on existentialism. I loved having those shared moments. I needed to return to that place of calm.

People were everywhere as I made my way. Left and right, I brushed up against another person, someone who wasn't paying attention, someone taking a photo, someone with a stroller, someone doing that influencer thing—you know, standing with baggy cargo pants on, iced coffee, plastic hair clip, oversized shirt, white Air Force 1s on with a tote bag, sunglasses half falling off their face. THESE people were everywhere. Didn't everybody know this was my time to walk the High Line in peace?

Despite the crowds, I passed the various side exit staircases. I needed to keep going to make it to THE spot. It's worth mentioning that past a certain point, you can't just turn around and easily get back down to street level. The platform with stairs to exit was quite a ways behind me, and the end of the High Line was still a half mile away. The section I entered was long, winding back and forth, through buildings budding up on each side. If there were places to dip back down, I was completely unaware of them. Walking between the long stretch with trees and high hedges, with buildings butting up right along the path, it felt like you were in a maze, only able to see a little ways up ahead.

With little to no warning, and unbeknownst to me, my urban adventure was about to go south. As I walked along, I barely noticed the sky becoming gray. I didn't think much about it, because in the Pacific Northwest every day is gray from October through May. It mists regularly and moisture comes down all the time. Gray is normal.

I learned real fast, however, that when it rains in New York City, it's as if the floodgates of a bathtub have been opened and Niagara Falls dumps on everyone in sight.

Like a tantrum from a three-year-old, the sky opened up and started a downpour as I hustled on the High Line. I looked up at the sky in shock—where did these clouds come from? How long was this going to last? As if with a snap of the fingers, the rain came down FAST and HARD. A storm hadn't been brewing, it just appeared out of nowhere, opened its eyes and started to cry. What was I to do? I had not yet made it to my favorite resting place. I didn't have an umbrella. Surely the rain would stop or let up soon. It couldn't Niagara Falls from the sky for more than a minute or two. Right?

Along with my lack of an umbrella, I wasn't wearing a rain jacket. And my trendy high-top Vans got soaked. My blistered feet went squish-squish as I pounded down on the path.

I was stuck. I didn't have any place to go to avoid the torrential downpour coming down. I didn't have a physical map and didn't want to pull out my phone in fear it would get soaked. Over the whole mile of upper rail line pathways, I knew only of a few staircases from which to exit. The steps down to street level were towards the beginning and there were only a few at the end. I would have to trek through the rain one way or the other. In a panicked moment looking for an escape, I found a maple tree and "hid" underneath some leaves to keep dry. That lasted for a few seconds. Why did I think I would be safe under a tree?

The people who had been moving pretty quickly earlier were suddenly nowhere to be found. I hope somebody from one of the buildings saw me standing there, looking confused under a maple tree. Someone must have seen me. I was HILARIOUS.

I took an unintentional shower in the middle of Manhattan with all my clothes still on.

I wrung out my T-shirt, gripped my shorts with my hands and squeezed out the water. It didn't matter, the damage had been done. I was a wet dog in the middle of August.

Thoughts kept running through my head about how I should

have turned around when I first saw those gray skies roll in. After a few minutes, I kept walking forward in search of a staircase, only to turn back around moments later. I did this a few times—back and forth I went, trying to determine where to go and what to do. I had this expectation inside of me that said *you have to recreate that first time experience.* The High Line was not just another destination to check off a list. I wanted to reconnect with those first feelings there, the moment I had. At the same time, it was pouring down rain, and I really needed to get dry.

See this idea that I had in my head, of needing to go back to THE spot and sit, enjoy the sights, take it all in—it just didn't happen. Even though I wanted to wait it out, I knew I had to take care of myself first. I needed to get out of the rain.

I did what anybody would have done—even if it took me a while. I ran back towards the end and took some stairs down. I found a gallery space to wring my clothes out for another round and then bolted to the nearest subway station.

I had not planned on getting stuck on a slick walkway in the middle of Manhattan. But there I was. Unable to stay dry. Drenched.

I started laughing. I started laughing when my underwear started to get wet. I was wet to my core.

Now, I think about how I so wanted to be back in that special place, sitting and looking out at the street below, believing THAT was where I was going to experience some sort of life change or peace. As the owner of a small business, there are many things that demand my attention. This hustle girlboss culture says if you aren't go-go-going all the time, then you aren't actually working enough. Exhibiting at this tradeshow in New York, I was trying to gain accounts, network with potential big box retailers, and promote my new products. For four solid days from 8 a.m. until 5 p.m. I was working at my booth, making small talk with hundreds of people, and trying to stay hydrated under intense fluorescent lights.

And even when the rain poured down, even after I decided to try to stick it out under a tree, I forced myself to keep going. I could have turned back sooner, but I was determined to get to where I was supposed to go until I was physically so wet that I had to find a stairway down to street level. I eventually stopped because I had to let go of this idea.

It is often the expectations and fears that can keep us stuck— not the circumstances themselves. A small mindset shift from panic to *you can figure this out*, a quick Google Maps search, and I could have gotten out of the rain sooner.

Storms do come. And we often have a destination in our lives we are trying to get to that those storms get in the way of. For whatever reason, we can be more focused on the desire to get there than taking in the information around us and accepting a slight detour. Usually it is in the process of getting there that the change and peace comes. Peace isn't found at the final location, but along the way. It comes in how we handle what is being poured on us.

A perspective shift offered by getting stuck in the rain reminded me that no matter what, I could get through my current challenges and make it to tomorrow. Getting Niagara Falls dumped on my head showed me that setting goals and getting to specific destinations is important, but so is enjoying the process. Even when cats and dogs are falling from the sky, we can stop and smile at a few of them.

HANG
TIGHT
THINGS
ARE GETTING
BETTER

CHECK IN ON YOURSELF

Find a tree, stand under it and set a timer for five minutes. Think about what protects you from the storms in your life.

_____

_____

_____

_____

_____

_____

_____

_____

_____

_____

_____

_____

_____

_____

_____

_____

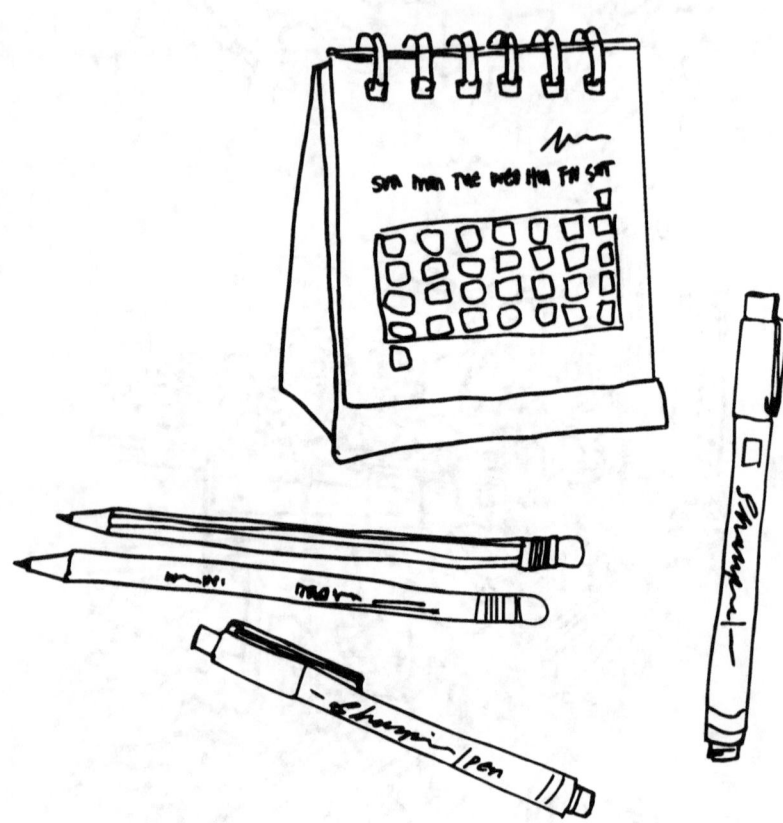

CHAPTER 4

All the Things

I was going back to school in the fall, but not as a student. With the leaves turning from green to red, yellow, and orange, I accepted a new job at Portland State University. I was to be an adjunct professor in the Graphic Design department, teaching three courses to undergraduate students. Two sections of an introduction class called Design Tools, helping students learn Adobe Photoshop and Illustrator. The third class was a silkscreen workshop, only one powerhouse weekend 9-5, three days in a row. I was half excited, jumping up and down, and half a nervous wreck, body sliding down onto the floor. *Did I have what it takes to teach the youth of America in this college capacity? Was I going to be able to perform and instruct effectively? Were the students going to like me? How do I even know what curriculum to teach?*

Thankfully, there were some meetings set up, Zoom calls, and discussions happening with the department lead and other professors who had taught these courses before. I was eager to soak up all they had to offer and the wisdom they were to share. I had taught college students back in graduate school, so I was familiar at least with this age group. But the digital pen tool via mouse or track pad is LIGHT YEARS different from fountain pen to textured paper. As more and more conversations happened over the

course of three weeks, I started to gain a better understanding of the content and lessons I would be teaching. If I am honest, it all scared the crap out of me. My background has always been in the fine arts, but I was being asked to rise to the occasion, dig in and learn more about these Adobe programs.

When I tell you that my stress level was at an all-time high, I need you to hear me tell you that the level got even higher as the beginning of the term neared. I was having a hard time shutting my brain off at night to fall asleep. Sleeping was not restful because I kept replaying the laundry list of things to get done the next day in my head. Instead of counting sheep I was counting tasks. This whole cycle was not sustainable. My nerves went from softly boiling water in a tea kettle to full on screeching and spilling over. I was trying to do all the things. Be the best well-prepared teacher, gain new design skills, network with new colleagues, and find my way around on a new campus. In hustle culture, it's okay if you are mentally, physically, and emotionally exhausted. It meant success in the eyes of the girlbosses. So when talking with friends or posting to social media, I was under the impression that being busy was somehow super important. So I stacked my schedule each day. *Starting something new ISN'T the least bit stressful. #sarcasm I just need to push forward and I can figure it out.* I raced the clock each day, cramming in as many things as I could.

When the term started, my weeks were all planned out for the next three months. Mondays and Wednesdays I would be on campus from 9 a.m. 'til 5 p.m., with a small break in between classes.

Tuesdays and Thursdays were for preparing and practicing the content I would be teaching the next week. I had projects to grade, daily emails to respond to, and this imposter syndrome to work through. *Nobody tells you how to manage all of your own insecurities. Can someone just stop the clock? I need a break.*

Having forty students twice a week and teaching the subject materials for the first time sent me reeling into TONS of self-doubt. *They can tell I am not good at this. They are judging me. I wish they didn't stare at me so much.* I was paralyzed reaching home from my bus ride each day for weeks. I wanted to be excellent at my new job but I didn't feel as though I measured up. I was putting so much pressure on myself. I thought I needed to know the answer to ALL of my student's questions, to direct them and guide them to be the next set of professional designers. These expectations were neither realistic nor attainable. But something inside of me said I must try at all costs. I was locked in a trap where my success was bound to doing more.

On top of the teaching each week I was running my own small business. I was grateful I had the flexibility to make my own hours and get this work done. After a day of teaching, I came home and posted up at my kitchen table double dipping—eating dinner while designing my next collection of greeting cards, managing supplies, updating my online sites, and packaging up orders for retail shops around the country. Plus I sold work at a local craft market on the weekends. To add to the workweek, I sometimes would substitute teach on Fridays just to earn some more money. With the amount of waking hours in a day, there just wasn't enough time to get it all done. I struggled to take care of myself. *Something's gotta give. You aren't going to be able to keep this all up.*

Usually if you speed ahead ten thousand miles per hour, you end up getting sick. I didn't actually get sick but something worse happened. I got shingles. And no I am not over fifty, quite the contrary. Waking up one Monday morning after my long three-day workshop weekend, I had pulled that Dolly Parton 9 to 5 schedule. I had taught my students how to transfer images onto screens, and expose, wash out, and print those images. It was beautifully exhausting. I was qualified and confident in this area, for I have been silk screening for over 10 years. But this Monday morning hit different. I started to realize I had some unlearning to do, stepping off the spinning wheel and needing to take a slower pace. To be busy was no longer serving me; it was harming me.

I looked down at my stomach and there were red rashes on my left side. *Where did these come from? Hello? What is happening?* Four distinct puffy pink continents wrapped around my belly button and moved up towards my natural waist. *I swear this is new for me.* Sometimes I get dry skin but this seemed like something different. *And yeah okay, they kind of burn when I touch them.* As I put on some jeans from my closet I noticed the waistband rubbed up against my skin causing some more irritation. As the day progressed I was reaching down to itch these troublesome areas. *Now I have little red bumps? Could this all be getting worse? How did I get this?*

Those spots on my stomach, the pain and the redness didn't go away fast. I had to slow down and let up on the stressors I was putting on myself. I was managing a lot of moving parts, but I needed to release the mental stress I was carrying. Nobody is meant to worry themselves to sickness. I did have a lot going on in my work days. I was trying to be available 24/7 for my students and run a successful business, but I was hitting burnout, spreading myself too thin. And my body knew it.

Somewhere in my weeks I tried to have a social life. My friend Kristin called me and asked to get together for a girl's night. As I shared my calendar, we realized the next open date was in *three months*. I was being pulled in so many directions and not seeing a break in sight for weeks down the road. After talking with her I realized how much pressure I was under, and much of it was from unrealistic expectations I had placed on myself. There is also this hustle culture pressuring everyone to be everything, all the time. I can add more to my already-full schedule.

Yet, in our modern world, our schedules are packed, and we still manage to find time to add more. So much pressure is put on women. Each of us can work all day, go to the grocery store, do laundry, and grab drinks with a friend who is visiting town. We work in workouts, call our parents, go on dates, make new recipes seen on TikTok, and attend sporting events. Kids soccer practice, daily yoga, volunteering, meal prepping, and taking a road trip all can lead to a full schedule. Getting sick happens, medical emergencies happen, and other stressors happen. Some weeks feel so stacked with house projects, long to-do lists, and meeting after meeting. There is pressure to fit a client call in before a long work day, happy hour before the concert, and hiking while all the seasonal wildflowers are in bloom. You have to make the most of your weekends, after all. With an emphasis on "you can have it all," and a hustle mentality, it leaves zero room for rest.

We have to preserve our energy and take back our calendars. Productivity paired with the current go-go-going mentality gives our schedules a full feeling. But what if the purpose is to commit to less? We need to push back on this hustle culture, to live as if we don't actually have to have it all. The intention should become saying yes to the things that add value to our days and not strain. To know where we can give our energy to and take the steps to confidently back away from the busyness.

When we commit to less, not always running from one thing to the next, we release the grip of unrealistic expectations. Whatever pace you are following and whatever value you assign to productivity, that is success, not what others are saying. I don't believe we can have a balanced life, but we can know when to stop, take a breath, and have check points within ourselves on how we are feeling.

No matter if you are transitioning into a new job, find yourself learning something new, or just noticing the seasonal changes in your life, you get to make choices in how you show up. And it is for you to decide what is important and what you need solely for yourself. Nobody else. Let go of the pressure and release those insecurities. They are not serving you. Trust me, shingles are not worth it.

TAKE ON THE DAY AND BREATHE

CHECK IN ON YOURSELF

Fill in this stylized week long calendar with three fun things you look forward to.

DATE __/__ — __/__

~ SUNDAY ~

☆ MONDAY ~

☺ TUESDAY ~

♡ WEDNESDAY ~

~ THURSDAY ~

☆ FRIDAY ~

~ SATURDAY ~

Use this space to draw out the good times.

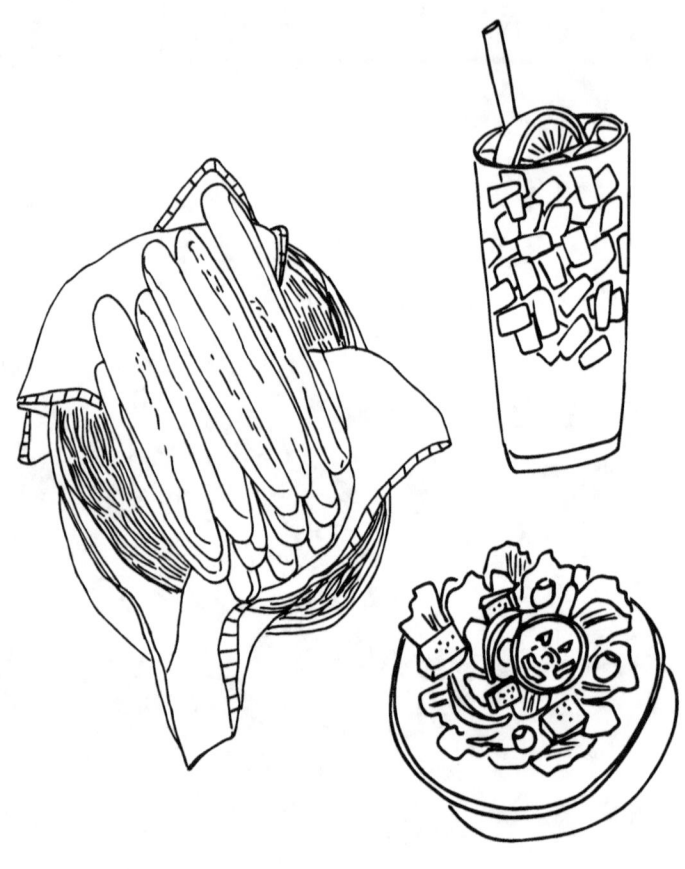

CHAPTER 5

One More Breadstick, Please

W hen the moon hits your eye like a big pizza pie, that's amore..."

Growing up, my siblings and I were allowed to pick any restaurant we wanted to go out to eat at for our birthdays. When it was my turn, I could go just about anywhere. I always picked Olive Garden, and so did my siblings.

The drive to Olive Garden took about 25 minutes. I reviewed the menu in my head before we even drove into the parking lot, but memorizing the entrees didn't get me out of my ordering ruts. I got the same thing birthday after birthday. For a few years it was the lasagna, then, the fettuccine alfredo, and finally, the Never Ending Pasta Bowl®. Baskets of breadsticks. At least two salads with that classic Olive Garden dressing. Raspberry lemonade. It seemed that nothing was off-limits for my birthday dinner.

Each year, after the never-ending main course, my mom or dad would whisper to our waiter that it was my birthday. The wait staff and even a loud group of chefs would spring out of the kitchen to sing, clap, and dance around a very small cake. As a preteen, the song and dance always embarrassed me quite a bit. A tiny cake was passed around the table and I took a tiny slice. Even this small dessert made my pants feel a little tighter.

On the drive home, the birthday excitement would wear off and my stomach would start to churn. I never felt quite right. As soon as I walked into the house, I would run upstairs. Every time without fail, the best birthday dinner had me in the bathroom.

I never remember anyone telling me about the effects of rich food on my system. I didn't know what was happening to my body in my post-birthday bathroom run. Because the salad and bread-sticks and raspberry lemonade were limitless, the idea was to have as much as I wanted. I did, but I destroyed my gut every time. I was miserable later, with a bloated stomach, cramping, and you got it, a big ol' number two.

Getting home after dinner I would take a look at myself in the mirror and didn't like how my stomach expanded. I had fun just hours before at my birthday dinner, but then I would get home and think there was something wrong with me when I looked in the mirror. Being bloated got me in a weird headspace. A young hormonal preteen can feel a lot of big feelings, but this mindset carried with me as I grew and matured.

Why get to know me with this story? Over the past few years, I have started to notice a practice I only half-intentionally began. It goes a little something like this: I wake up in the morning and look at myself in the mirror. And I like how I look.

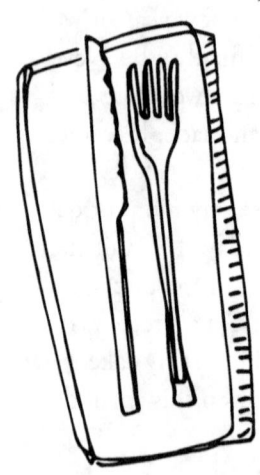

Everything in my mind is cheering, thoughts do happy dances around my cerebral cortex. I take note of my middle section, notice how flat it is and how my pants hit my waist. But by midday or after dinner, I am in front of that same mirror in complete shock that my stomach has grown about five times bigger. That inner voice reappears and tells me something is wrong with me. Had I perceived incorrectly earlier? My pants feel tighter (even though it isn't my birth-day and there have been no lemonade or unlimited breadsticks). My mind shifts from morning party to emo garbage about my midday body. I could have accomplished summiting a freakin mountain that day and I still can't even hold space for that joy. It is always squashed with a fear that somehow I am doing something wrong.

Don't eat that again! The workout you did wasn't enough, like, you didn't even sweat enough! This inner voice comes in loud and clear, throwing insults at the choices I made. I start stressing over the calories in the food. The carbs are not "good" for me and I ate "too many" in that meal. Food was grabbed out of comfort and later made me feel unhappy. Have you ever felt like the day was a waste, that you got off track if you started with a donut and then found yourself having ice cream later, then cocktails with friends, and then late-night pizza? I crave those things every month, sometimes stronger than others. Then, my brain logs how I feel and I make impulse assumptions that I am not living up to the discipline of making "good" choices.

Or my personal favorite,

"If you want a guy to like you, you are going to have to fix that muffin top!"

Seriously, these are horse-shit lies. We need to accept this fact: everyBODY gets bloated. Let that dance party resume. No food is intrinsically bad, and in moderation you can have the cheeseburger, the candy, the fill in the blank.

Because guess what? We get bloated—no matter what.

THIS IS NORMAL. Let me repeat....we all experience bloating, and it is normal. Bloating means that you have food in your body and that your stomach is working to digest it, to use it for fuel. As I have researched and talked with many friends, I've learned we all experience the expanding and contracting of our middle sections.

It is time we stop comparing ourselves to what we think we

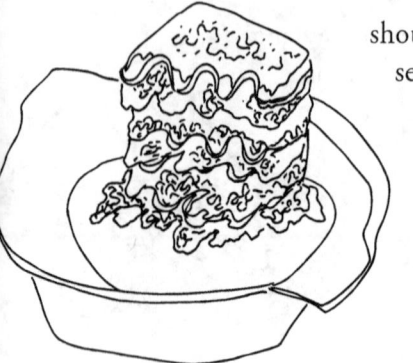

should look like. It's time to love the vessel we were given, bloat and all. I have come to this realization because the filters on social media aren't realistically portraying our bodies, dieting isn't sustainable, and the older my body gets, my metabolism needs me to be kind to myself. This one-two punch approach only causes me anxiety and stress when I eat. My mind got a reset when I would snap a selfie at the start of my day to when I would snap a pic later. If I couldn't love myself fully, for all my soft parts and squishy layers, then all the compliments sharing those first pictures didn't matter. I was created to encourage others and I wasn't speaking with that same tone with myself. It gets tiring to always be worrying about your middle area.

How many times have you stood in front of the mirror looking at yourself when you wake up in the morning, checking in on your stomach? Then, later in the afternoon, checking in again, noticing you grew a few belly sizes? It can really get us down. Especially as we get older, or when pants don't fit the same, lies start to creep in that we aren't working out enough, that we somehow got the worst genetics, or that we simply aren't as valuable if we are larger.

Going out to eat at Olive Garden is fun and celebrating who we are is good. We get bloated. It happens. Of course, it's important to check in with our bodies, to listen, to feel our best, but it's also wise not to feel guilty when we indulge a bit. It is okay to enjoy, knowing we might get bloated later. It's okay to love our bodies at any size, at any time of day. I am still working on not being so hard on myself in this area. Grab that glass of wine if you desire and enjoy it.

"When the world seems to shine
like you've had too much wine, that's amore!"

EVERY BODY GETS BLOATED

CHECK IN ON YOURSELF

Draw out your favorite meal below:

WHAT FOODS DO YOU ENJOY EATING?

_____

_____

_____

_____

_____

_____

_____

_____

_____

_____

_____

_____

_____

HOW DO THEY MAKE YOU FEEL?

_____

_____

_____

_____

_____

_____

_____

_____

_____

_____

_____

_____

_____

_____

CHAPTER 6

One Atypical Tulip

There's something so beautiful about opening up and being vulnerable, even if it means being different.

Tulips are my favorite spring flower. I am always caught off guard when they "spring up" in the florist section as I enter the store. One day in early spring, I saw them on sale at the local grocery store. Walking towards the display, I was struck by the bold reds, yellows, oranges, and soft purples. A sign read "four dollars per bunch," and so I went back and forth to decide which color I wanted to take home with me. Reaching for the soft violet ones, I placed them inside my cart and carried on buying the rest of my items. Excitedly, I got home and placed the tulips in a vase. I turned on the faucet too quickly and SPLASH, water went over the sides, not realizing how suddenly I plunged the stems in. I set the vase near the window hoping the petals would open. But I knew I was going to have to wait patiently. Tulips gravitate toward the light on their own schedule.

Tulips remind me of the beauty that comes out of the ground after a long season of waiting. I waited a little bit longer even after those bulbs rose from the earth and rested in a container at my house. Oftentimes I have found who I am becoming in the ground. The growth and challenges of maturing into the woman I want to be versus who the world expects me to be are hard. The color that can come from living a life that is fully and wholly yours is one that takes risk and courage. There have been many times I didn't know what choices to make. What was buried in the ground, inside of my heart, seemed very hidden.

In a clear glass vase, the tulips sat. They slowly rose towards the sun's rays and I waited for any movement on their part. Not a petal started to open. So I waited. I waited and I waited some more. After about four days one tulip was not like the others. Eleven of twelve headed straight up as tall as they could muster. Quietly, like a secret written in a poetic phrase, one tulip made up its mind. It was taking a different path. Reaching and extending beyond the glass rim, she angled out to the right, horizontal not vertical, lower and more intentional than the rest.

There must have been better light coming from another window in my living room. I tried to fix the "problem" of my tilted tulip, because in my opinion, this flower shouldn't be doing what it was doing. The purple tulip should be like the others, rising right up, standing tall in this vase, as flowers do.

But maybe beauty is not about doing what one is supposed to do. We can take up space onto a different path and still be beautiful. We can feel stuck in what we are contained in or conformed to (by our world or our circumstances), but we too can find the strength to do our own thing, go our own way, and make our own choices. Comparison can keep us from really becoming who we are meant to become. When we focus on everyone else, we miss being our true authentic selves. Simply and quietly, this tulip has reminded me that I have to drop the "shoulds," and just do what I was designed to do. BOOM like magic after a few more days, the tulips opened up. The petals revealed their full color.

There are so many expectations I am trying to live by, placed on me from others. I care what people think of me. I want to make my parents proud. I don't want to let anybody down. Our minds can be so inundated by what we should be producing, what we should be accomplishing, what we ought to be feeling. This pressure can cause us to feel lonely or uneasy when we choose a different path.

I can choose something different.

I really struggle to do this. I want people to like me. I want people to understand me. But I don't need to conform to the thought patterns that keep me small or knock me down if I am not on the "right" path. In the decisions I am making I want to say HELL YES to opportunities that cause me to shine and stick my neck out. When others around you are growing and moving in a certain direction, it is okay and necessary to go your own way. Your inner color will be revealed stronger, brighter, and true to who you are becoming. I don't want to worry about what everybody thinks or what others are up to.

No matter what, when we compare ourselves and our experiences to others, it can keep us from becoming who we are meant to be. People may see where you are and what you are up against and be concerned. But you just have to keep being you and go in the direction you are being led in. Extend as far out of that vase as you can, babe. You got this.

YOU ARE SERIOUSLY SOOOOO BEAUTIFUL

CHECK IN ON YOURSELF

Buy a bouquet of your favorite flowers. Sketch out the different stages throughout the week.

CHAPTER 7

Tying Shoes and Chasing Sunsets

I arrived in Reykjavík, Iceland, for my first ever International Art Residency. I was about to spend the next month creating alongside other artists. It was a trip of my dreams. There was no agenda but to make a bunch of art and share it in an exhibition at the end of the month.

Before I even set foot in my new room and studio, I was already doubting myself. Thoughts swirled in my head about how hard it was to get into this program, and how I didn't get in the first time I applied. Rejection stings, but I knew there must have been reasons for the decisions the committee made. *Why was I accepted this time? Was I supposed to be here?*

Standing in the white blank-walled room, feelings of inadequacy seeped into my head. I was not an accomplished ceramicist, not an exquisite oil painter, not a realist portraitist, I was JUST an illustrator. I had proposed a specific project and feared I was not going to be able to accomplish what I set out to do. *Was anybody going to care if the work I proposed in my application changed?*

Though I was excited to be there, I was also very overwhelmed. It was a huge privilege to step away from my business back in Portland, to pursue with intentionality my own art practice. To have time set apart to create exactly what I wanted. But for some reason, this pressure welled up inside and it started to feel debilitating.

My room looked out at the ocean with land jutting out into the sky off in the distance. Setting my keys down, I unpacked all of my items from my carry-on and suitcase. One by one, I met new artist friends from all over the world. It was all very exciting. I wondered if they would like my work. I started a routine, getting outside every day to take a walk. Sometimes I went downtown to buy a cinnamon roll, and sometimes I lightly jogged along a path that extended around the water.

One day, upon waking up, I peeled myself out of bed to look outside and it appeared to be windy with a chance of slightly stormy skies. Opening my window just a crack, I reached my hand out and tried to feel out what clothes I should wear. I needed to get some fresh air, to get out and move my body. I decided to go for a run, my first run in Iceland. Let's be clear, running is not my favorite, but I was committed to self-improvement for my body and mind on this trip. This included going outside, and sometimes even running. I didn't have access to a gym, so letting my legs and muscles move was important.

As I tied my tennis shoes and slipped my black fleece over my head, I decided not to wear a jacket. I wanted to feel the moisture on my neck and face. It appeared to be lightly raining and I didn't mind it. With thoughts of inadequacy as an artist surfacing, I figured I would just have to prove to myself that I had what it took to succeed at this art residency. I was already an artist, but I needed a reminder that I could believe in myself and grow into more of who I desired. Apparently running was a metaphor for this. Showing up and getting outside—bringing out what you know is already inside of you. Making my way down a couple flights of stairs, I pulled the front metal door open. Double-checking I had my key to get back in, I let the heavy door close behind me. I noticed my right sock starting to bother me; I just couldn't be bothered to fix it.

The art residency was situated on Seljavegur street overlooking the water. To make sure I could find my way back I jotted down the name of this street, for visual landmarks and street signs are helpful markers. Spelling it correctly, S-e-l-j-a-v-e-g-u-r, so I could Google Map it later if needed. While on the cement sidewalk, I would make my way to the main road from the side streets.

Crossing over a major road near the water, my journey would really start at the shore's edge. Being close to the ocean always had a way of bringing up my internal feelings. The vast expanse put things into perspective, causing me to feel most alive. The path was a paved snake-shaped walkway that followed the shore. Weather patterns in Iceland caused the atmosphere to be very ominous, with the sky opening up to rain for a little bit. Some days the clouds would move in very fast. I looked down at my feet and then out at the ground ahead. It was time to begin. I was ready. Feet hitting the pavement, I started out slow, focusing on my breathing as I placed each foot on the ground. I was grateful I brought my Adidas tennis shoes with the extra cushion.

If you saw me out there, I am not sure you would call it running. But I was trying. Starting and stopping. Stretching my calf muscles, reaching my arms up over my head to bend them down along my sides. I angled my body over upon itself folding in half, to slowly be straight up again. Standing on my tip toes, giving room for my heels to stop burning and release the tension being placed on them. Many times in the first mile I walked at a good pace, to run for a minute, and back to walking some more. The water brought a cool breeze which hit my face and my hair was whipping around my neck. I wasn't worried about the light rain getting my head wet.

I took my little mini iPod Shuffle with me, which I had just downloaded a new album onto. *Good Luck Kid* by The Band Joseph. A song called "Half Truths" came on. I hit repeat. The drums always got me into a good rhythm, steady and focused. As the chorus came in with the line "I've got half a mind to lose… I've got half a mind to soothe…," I felt my eyes start to tear up. It brought out an understanding of how I had worked so hard to get to this place, but why was I also doubting my worth? My mind was for me and against me. I was battling what I needed to let go of and how to be kind to myself. The lyrics continued, "Just how many half truths do I have to tell myself to get through?" And I didn't just repeat this song a few times. I would hit repeat constantly over the next 72 hours. I let the melody, the harmonies, and the lyrics wash over me. It was a real banger that hit a chord inside my chest. In the bridge of the song specifically, it mentions the half-truths we tell ourselves to get through. *Was I good enough to be in this program? I didn't get in the first time, so why now? What was I actually going to create? I am not a runner, so why am I going to try?* These ideas all ruminated inside of my mind as I rounded the first corner. Ever heard the phrase "fake it til you make it?"

As I continued on mile two of my run, I noticed multiple metal benches to the left with some apartment structures. The clouds kept shifting and changing above. Birds hovered and squawked overhead to let me know they owned the air. Tall grasses waved alongside me and I passed by a natural hot spring pool fit for one. A little hidden gem next to a small green structure. I felt grateful to be out in nature but worried about the paved path ahead, how it stretched out for miles. With the song still repeating, I tried to run to the beat as my eyes swelled up with tears. I so desperately wanted to feel more alive.

I thought more about the parallels between running and my art—the half-truths I had believed about both. *Here we go, keep a good pace, move those feet.* Even though I would not characterize myself as a runner, I needed to try. *Moving forward, let's go.* There was no need to worry about the outcome, it was all about showing up. *Focus on what is ahead. You got this.* To get outside, to move my body, and start and stop whenever I needed to. *Yeah! We are out here lightly jogging. Look at you fly.* I was on the hunt to recalibrate my intentions and thoughts about what it meant to be present in these next four weeks. Nobody was going to be able to make the art for me. I had to believe in the whole process, from picking up my pen and drawing. I would not be an imposter working in my studio. I was selected, chosen, and accepted into this space. I needed to trust I could succeed. *Feet slowing down, stopping, pausing. Take in a few deep breaths. Inhale, now exhale.* Deep breaths and already achy knees, I paused on the trail noticing a lighthouse around the corner. I wondered what it would be like to run there one day—to touch it. The lighthouse seemed so far away, but I wanted to reach it. I hoped I could get there.

Multiple times I had to stop on my first run on that September morning. It was rough. I cried a handful of times. I would get a cramp in my shin, or my shoe lace would come untied, or I stopped at a natural rock drinking fountain to take a sip. The path was pretty flat and the only people I encountered were older couples walking their dogs. But everyone smiled as they passed me. No one was judging me harder than myself.

Like running on a path, there was a journey I was on with my art-making, a process of becoming. I knew I was good enough to be at this art residency, not because of a committee choosing me, but because I showed up. The skills I needed to complete the work ahead of me were already within me. I had to create and believe in the process. Just as I reached for my tennis shoes that first morning run, I needed to reach for my pen and sketchbook. The work was not going to make itself. I had been given a truly unique opportunity to create art in Iceland alongside other artists. It was time to take the pressure off myself, let go of the self-doubt and leave it at the shoreline. Blessings were washing up along the path I was headed on. Perfectionism needed to be released so I could be freed up to grow.

I made it a personal goal before the end of the month that I was going to run straight up to the lighthouse. With some practice and discipline, stretching, and maybe a slower steady pace, I figured I could get there. A four mile stretch, not stopping, with the intent of not giving up on myself. Putting on my tennis shoes for morning and afternoon runs in the rain, I would touch that base of the lighthouse structure. I was ready to chase those sunsets.

BEING PRESENT IS LIFE-GIVING

CHECK IN ON YOURSELF

Write out the lyrics to your favorite song.

_____

_____

_____

_____

_____

_____

_____

_____

_____

_____

_____

_____

_____

_____

_____

Draw out some of your favorite albums and singers.

CHAPTER 8

Eating the Whole Chocolate Bar

I stepped into a New Seasons grocery store, a local chain here in Portland, Oregon. I was immediately greeted by a friendly employee wearing a dozen enamel pins on their apron. When you know a grocery store like the back of your hand, you can find your items fast. My eyes moved quickly over to the third aisle. Passing by a fruit stand, coffee bags on display, and some journals, I rounded the corner into the chocolate sale section. Every year, around the Hallmark holiday in February, otherwise known as Valentine's Day, New Seasons marks down all their chocolate bars. What a great day to celebrate love and thank you for discounting all of the chocolate. *Would anybody notice I was only buying chocolate? Why did this feel like a bad idea?*

Standing in the aisle, with eight-foot tall rows and rows and rows of boxes of chocolate before me, I started researching my options. I wanted to get the best deals. The very top rows had local truffles, the middle rows were filled with environmentally safe chocolates and a brand that has poems in the wrapper. Further down were the peanut and nut butter cups with a bunch of toffees, caramels, and pretzel varieties. From milk and dark chocolate, to salted almonds, mint, and rose petals, it all sounded so good. I was going to buy a few different bars. I thought it would be fun to try a variety of kinds to see which was my favorite. I am a sucker for good branding. I will pick something just because it looks cool or the packaging is well-designed.

Stretching my 5'5" body, rising to my tiptoes, and reaching for the top shelf was tricky. I lost my balance and fell over. All of the New Seasons male employees are quite handsome, so you gosh darn better believe I asked for some assistance. I looked over all my options, scouring up and down for the perfect chocolate. Reading labels and looking into all the ingredients, I was struck by ALL THE SUGAR. *How could something so good be so bad for you? Was it okay to buy more than two bars?*

Bending down, as if a spotlight had been turned on, I saw all the Tony's Chocolonely chocolate bars—the red bar, blue bar, orange bar, lime green bar, dark green bar, and purple bar. These are easily three times the size of all the others. I pulled the milk chocolate hazelnut to my chest, I honestly felt like I won gold. It's like I was at Willy Wonka's chocolate factory and I'd been given the biggest gift of all! Tony's brand did a fantastic job of calling me and reminding me that this is what I needed RIGHT now.

But then, I read the ingredients. WOW. Not the most nutrient rich item. The debate started inside my mind like a runaway freight train. *This is a bad decision. You are making a poor choice right now. Step back, move away. You don't need this.*

Handing the chocolate over to the register, I swiped my card and exited the store. I bought the biggest chocolate bar there was. Weighing in my hands, heavier than a block of cement, I found what I came for.

I figured since I walked to the grocery store, I earned these calories. While walking home, I ate a few squares.

I opened up the foil, put the bar into my hands, heard the paper

break it apart

wrapper twist, and then all of a sudden, cue the choir of angels, cue Cupid, and all the love in the world. I broke off more squares. We were doing this.

But as I ate and walked, I looked at the calories almost incessantly, counting as I ate them, thinking how "bad" for me things were going inside my body. I started to spiral. I let this negative train of thought run faster than I could even imagine. At a mile a minute, I thought about *how bad of an idea this is, I shouldn't be doing this.* The other half of me said, *treat yourself, this is the best thing for you right now, and your body wants the sugar. Don't be disciplined, go all in, it's just a chocolate bar.* I couldn't even enjoy the chocolate bar that I was so excited to get just a half hour before.

But then I realized that it's not even about just a chocolate bar. I found that it really was about finding a piece of comfort. I kept aimlessly snatching another chunk of chocolate to distract myself to feel a sense of comfort from the loneliness and discontentment. The sugar hit my tastebuds, firing off dendrites to make a connection in my brain that this was pleasurable. In the same thread though, this chocolate shopping trip sent me into a spiral motion that I was doing something wrong. I was not doing something good for my body, therefore not taking care of myself.

At home, I immediately peeled more of the paper wrapper away, only letting myself have a square. As I put away other items from my errand run, I grabbed another square of chocolate. Starting on some work, I got distracted by a phone call and found myself back at the chocolate bar breaking off another square as I chatted. Each time I would reach for another piece to nibble on, I told myself this was the last one for today, but by the end of the day, I had aimlessly eaten the whole bar. A huge wave of guilt came over me. *How did I eat that whole bar? You shouldn't have gone through that whole bar so fast. What even was the flavor? Don't buy chocolate again!* Over time I realized I needed to stop punishing myself because it was hurting me on the inside. I was tired of feeling exhausted from the mental rat race.

Recently I have landed in a new practice where I buy chocolate to really sit down and enjoy it. This came about because I let go of the distractions around me. The point was to savor the cocoa, sugar, and milky flavors as they go down. Slowing down and letting it be the only thing that I'm doing stops the accusatory mental game. I found that an empty wrapper before me now just signifies that I really relished in something and am in a healthier place mentally because of it.

Eating chocolate isn't bad for you. And I am aware that some people may have a more troubled relationship with food. Even reading a story like this can bring up some hard things. Yet, I might argue that the negative self-talk spiraling around in my mind was more harmful to my body than eating the bar. Thoughts and guilt only leave us feeling more hurt. Watching calorie intake and being disciplined with food choices are important, and what I am suggesting is that choosing to unwrap a favorite bar of chocolate can be a pleasurable thing. We can have mindful indulgence. I encourage you to sit and enjoy the flavors landing in your mouth. To be aware and take a pause from any other activity. You can take the time for something as simple as relishing in a treat for yourself. It is a beautiful thing. It is okay and it is important to allow yourself such simple pleasures in life. Let it be worth it.

BUY THE CHOCOLATE

CHECK IN ON YOURSELF

Buy your favorite snack, and draw it out in different stages.

Decide how you want to eat it—slowly versus all at once—and reflect on how awesome the snack is using mindfulness techniques.

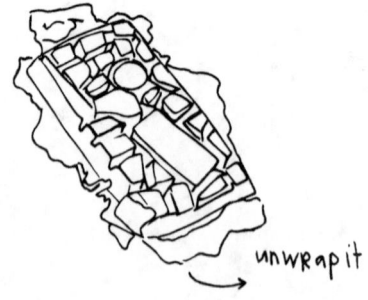

unwrap it

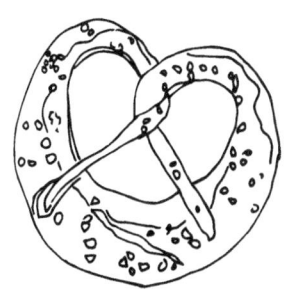

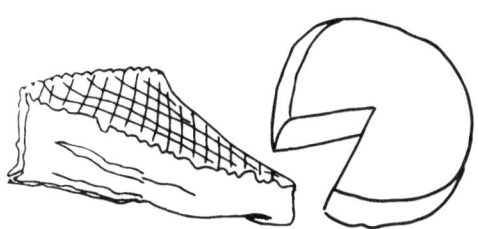

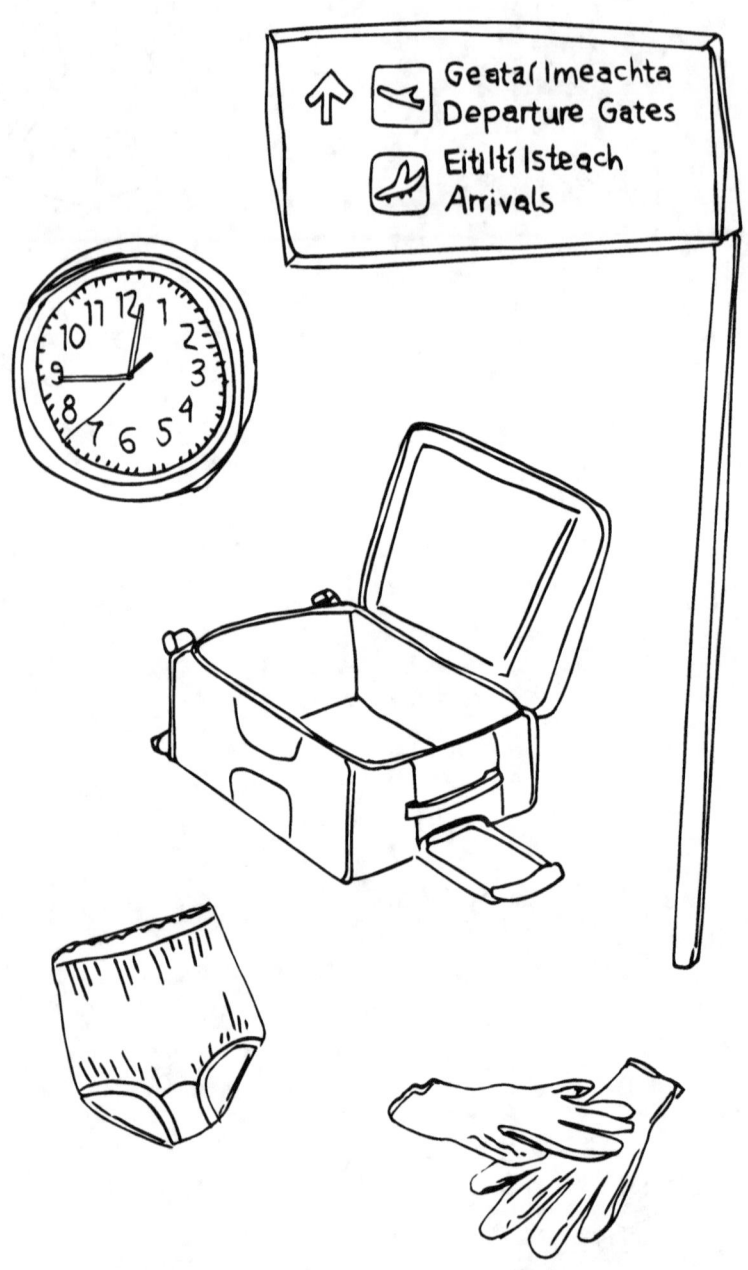

CHAPTER 9

Loosen Your Grip

Excuse me, miss, you're going to have to step over here. We are going to check a few things. Is this your bag?" *Ugh, what? Is this really happening? Why does this gentleman have to go through my suitcase?*

"What do you need? What? You're talking to me? Oh, OK?" I mumbled half-asleep as I looked up at this person telling me to step aside.

Hello, you gorgeous blue-eyed Irish man wearing that TSA neon yellow security vest. Welcome to the Dublin International Airport. It dawned on me that maybe I had just unintentionally stepped into the set of a movie. *Were we the lead characters about to fall in love?* I straightened up and looked more awake. Damn, he was attractive. I hoped he couldn't smell my terrible travel breath. My heart started to race as I stared at this man, allowing the stress of the unknown to enter my mind at the same time. *Was I going to miss my connecting flight?!*

Let me rewind this story back to the start of my 28 hour travel day that felt like a living nightmare.

The summer sun beat down on my rust-orange floral dress. I indulged in another piece of homemade blueberry cheesecake. Wine in hand, I gave a "cheers" with my Kiwi/New Zealand friend

Josiah while watching the setting sun. The air smelled of cows, hay, and sweet wildflowers. I had traveled to the countryside in the Netherlands for a friend's wedding. Everyone danced the night away in a beautifully decorated barn. We had the time of our lives at this international celebration. I was to sleep a few winks before taking a train out in the morning back to Amsterdam. I was going to miss this property, animals, and bike paths we frequented over the past week on the farm in Eelde.

After saying goodbye to dear friends Michael and Taylor in the morning, I was dropped off at the train station in Groningen. I was headed back to Amsterdam to spend one last night before I took an early morning flight the next day. Riding the train for just under two hours, I felt relaxed, super happy, and excited to try a popular pizza spot for dinner.

I got off the train and walked about fifteen minutes to my Airbnb and was greeted by the nicest host, who happened to be originally from Boston. He showed me to my room. It was perfect and quaint. I opened the window, flopped down on the white linen bed, and enjoyed the view. Taking a few deep breaths in, I felt so grateful for this lovely room and city I had come to fall in love with. Everything was going so well and I was sad to be leaving. Setting my alarm for 4:15 a.m., I had an Uber ride ordered for 4:30 a.m. All I had to do was wake up, roll out of bed, and get down some steep stairs to the car.

Before I knew it, bell tower chimes WOKE me from my peaceful sleep and BAM I didn't feel very calm anymore. Normally, there is a lingering nervousness around traveling for me. The day was going to be a long one, with many moving parts, and I hoped it would (crossing my fingers) all work out.

I anxiously waited for my Uber. Due to travel restrictions, I was told to give myself at least four hours at the airport to get through security, check in, and get to my gate. The world was getting back on track after being shut down for so long, but I found that most things weren't completely back to normal. Luckily, I didn't need to be checked for vaccination or prove a negative Covid test. Many said I could get to my final destination with ease. NOTHING about this early morning felt easy.

When the Uber driver arrived, we took off so rapidly I nearly lost my dinner from the previous night. I was having a terrible bout of IBS and was super sick the night before. This too can be standard for me, but I did feel like I was coming down with some stomach bug. The Uber driver got me to the airport in record-breaking speeding ass time. By the time he dropped me off, I felt super woozy and tried to locate where I needed to go next.

Bombarded with different signs, people dragging suitcases in different directions, and all the different lines for every airline, I found myself in chaos. Clenching my jaw, I maneuvered my suitcase through it all in 15 minutes. *What was I going to do with the next three hours before I boarded the plane to Ireland?* I desperately needed to rest and figured I could sleep a little. I found a hard couch and rubbed my stomach. Everything was going to go smoothly from here. Layover number one will be chill.

TURN AND TWIST, my body was curled up in the fetal position on that gray bench with silver metal armrests. Tension gave way in my stomach causing a fight between my large and small intestines. *Did I eat something bad at the wedding? Was this issue happening because of no sleep?* There was no part of me that was looking forward to the next flight.

In order to get back home to Portland, Oregon, I would have a flight to Dublin, Ireland, and then a second flight out of Dallas, Texas to my home once I landed in the U.S. The cheapest option doesn't always mean the best option. WOOF. *Why did I pick this path for myself? Take a deep breath. Inhale and exhale. Do it again.*

Because I was in Ireland for over one minute, I needed to be vetted into their country, which I didn't know previously. Did I mention I was also exhausted? At this point, I had been awake for X AMOUNT of hours, had celebrated a friend's wedding, and was still battling stomach pains. Here's how it happened: I got to the security line once we landed in Ireland, and I showed my passport and boarding pass, which was standard. Check. Zero sleep in me meant that I had zero patience in me. Check. Navigating a new system at six in the morning was not something I was prepared for. Check.

One line brought me to the next. The Ziploc bag requirement. Shit. Many of my bottles were in multiple different portions of my suitcase. I tried my best but I was slowly freaking out, FRANTI-CALLY shoving bottles into clear bags. Check. My body physically started to shake. *Was I going to get in trouble? Was I doing this correctly? How much time did I have? I can't miss my flight!* I got obnoxiously worried and didn't know how to calm my body down. My inner temperature flared up causing me to sweat. I had momentarily lost my ability to think clearly and cope with the rising stress.

Then it happened. You know what I'm talking about—the part when you take your shoes off, placing your jacket and bags on the conveyor belt as it all gets scanned by who knows what kind of camera system. The low hum of the machine could be calming white noise until it beeps and an alarm goes off. You don't even understand what that all means and you gosh darn hope it's not your stuff getting flagged.

But it was my lucky day. BEEP! They started pulling my stuff.

Let's get back to the hunk of an Irish security gentleman shall we?!

"Yes, Miss. You see there are things in this bag that we need to check and go through. We must make sure that you can have them."

I looked at him through my tired eyes and felt an instant

chemistry. He was so attractive but I held it together. CHURN CHURN POUND rolled my gut a few times.

In agreement, I said, "OK do whatever you need to do."

I looked into his eyes. I saw kindness and compassion, but I also saw a man who was just trying to do his job. I don't blame him, nor was I mad at him. I was just frustrated that it was 6 A.M. and somebody was going through my stuff. So there I was with tired eyes and holding my shoes in my hand. The Irish security officer put on blue latex gloves, unzipped my rolling carry-on, and started pulling things out one by one. I start chuckling even now just thinking about this moment. He proceeded with some nice conversation, "how are you doing" and I say "oh I'm good, I am a little tired." I was not prepared for what was to happen next.

Then I saw it, in his right blue latex glove, he pulled out my underwear, my dirty underwear. There's the black pair! Oh, he reached and then he pulled out the black and white striped pair! Oh and there was that mint green pair! Oh he got the gray pair next. Then another pair, another pair, another pair. Stacked in his hands, moving from blue latex gloves into a gray bin. *Was everybody seeing my dirty underwear? Does he always hold ladies underwear?* A wave of embarrassment rolled through my head. Scanning the room I looked left, then to my right and made eye contact with a sixty five-year-old Irish woman in a wheelchair. She started shaking her head and it was as if we were thinking the same thing. How ridiculous that my underwear was out for all to see. Next to me, another American girl was getting her bag searched too. She looked shocked and comforted that I was already going through the process.

Looking at this Irish man, I couldn't help but to say, "So, you see this is pretty comical! I am writing a book and I need you to know that this story is going to go in the book." My dirty underwear was piling high in the gray bin now as the sentences came out.

"Oh what's your book about?"

"Oh it's for women, stories about life, overcoming things, and having hope." *Maybe how to remain calm when your stuff is being rifled through.*

"Good luck on your book."

I never got his name nor did I want it, but he looked at me with all my dirty underwear just resting in the bin next to him. With all my other stuff he said, "I'm just going to take THIS back and run it through. Wait here, I'll be back."

"OK," I mustered up to say. I couldn't believe that my dirty underwear was out for all to see. It felt like all of my insecurities and vulnerabilities were on display. Not only for me but for a beautiful man on a random morning in an airport. He came back and he gave me the bin and said, "It's all good. Hope you have a great day. Good luck on your book!"

I just remember at that moment how I wanted to purchase all new underwear. Such depth of embarrassment having a gorgeous man see my things. I needed to upgrade my cottons to lace! I'm laughing at telling the story because I don't know if you understand the intensity of uneasiness that I felt in those minutes. It wasn't just any security guy. I had to get the attractive, the chiseled, the I-want-to-make-out-with-you kind. As if we were in a movie. Now the beautiful stranger knew what my underwear looked like. Was I supposed to feel sexy still moving forward? STOMACH PAINS, TWISTING, BURNING. Also, I made note that next time I would be investing in direct flights to go from A to B, instead of A to B to C back to A. That sounded like a better choice for my next international trip.

Stuffing everything as fast as I could into my suitcase, I rushed down some stairs where I had to go through another line of security. To enter back into my homeland, flying into Texas before my flight to Portland, I needed clearance from the American government. Yippee!

MacGyvering new airports, having multiple connecting flights, with long travel days through multiple time zone changes is enough to send anybody into a tizzy. It all can be tricky to navigate while security officers are seemingly looking over your shoulder, needing to find food to eat and restrooms to freshen up in. You are fending for yourself and it can get stressful.

It's okay to be a little lost in the process and for your body tension to rise. With many things out of your control in these situations, it can be hard to remember to breathe.

Looking back on this experience, I wished I could have given myself some kindness. Numerous times all I wanted to do was give up and start crying. Now, I wish that I could have embraced the mess of the situation, chuckling more at myself for all that I packed in that suitcase. I really should have gotten the guy's email, Instagram, something.

The way forward when stress starts to hit involves centering my breath, pausing what I am doing, and taking a sip of my water. This mental pause allows me to reassess for a minute and then take a peace-filled minute to pray. By doing this I become centered and it helps me let go of the turmoil. Traveling can be stressful. Just make sure all your bottles fit into one Ziploc bag. It will definitely help, unless you want to talk to a good-looking security officer.

GIVE YOURSELF A BRIEF MOMENT

CHECK IN ON YOURSELF

When stress and tensions rise, where do you find your peace and become calm? Write out different ways to shift your mindset for when those tough situations come calling.

_____

_____

_____

_____

_____

_____

_____

_____

_____

_____

_____

_____

_____

_____

_____

_____

CHAPTER 10

Sweaty Face Wipe on Hot Guy's T-Shirt

It was the night. You could feel it in the air. It was warm. It was summer, and it was time to go out dancing. I was hopeful for a romantic connection, even if it was just for the night on the dance floor. There is something so freeing to put that intention out there and see where the night could go. I couldn't wait! A few girlfriends and I had decided earlier in the week that on Friday we were going to hit the local bar, Dig-a-Pony, to find ourselves between some hip hop beats and some good-looking fellas. This bar is not known for 100% quality men, but I don't think any bar can deliver 100% in that category.

When we go out dancing, as a group of girls, there's usually a couple of weirdos who get a little handsy and aren't there for the right reasons. They just want to get drunk and make it more than a PG-13 type of night. You have to dodge the grinders and be smart while having a night out.

I think part of the anticipation of moving my body and seeing if I found myself dancing the night away is that this feeling was a new one for me. After growing up in a purity culture movement that told girls not to get too close to guys, not to cause them to

"sin," that if we did rub up against anyone we would be commit-
ting something terrible in God's eyes. I wasn't saying "to hell" with
that old college mentality, but I had been stepping into a new-
found freedom that gave me agency over my own body. I could
make choices that were best for me and it was quite alright with
God if I got a little close with a guy. Stepping into the bar that
night, I wanted to be seen and feel close to someone. Nothing
wrong with embracing some attraction on the dance floor.

Earlier while getting ready, I started to braid the left top section
of my hair, pinning back some of my wild curls, completing my
going-out attire. I was wearing my freckles and a gold heart locket
necklace from my grandmother. I had on a mint crop top tank
that was tight and high-waisted black shorts that were a little short.
Don't worry, my butt wasn't hanging out. I rocked my black high-
top Vans with just a little sock sticking out the top. I felt ready and
sexy. My credit card and ID were tucked into my right sock and
my phone was in my back pocket, keys attached to the loop on my
shorts with an orange carabiner (not suitable for climbing).

My two girlfriends got in line as I parked the car. Stepping into
the bar, we immediately ordered a drink. With my gin and tonic
in hand, I looked around the room. The bar was already popping
with lots of people. The noise level rose as people started drinking. The time was nearing 10:30 p.m. and the DJ started spinning
those old-school hip hop songs. Mixing one into the next, some

folks started to find their way over to
the smallest dance floor in Portlandia. The floor was white-tiled
with black grout, which would
not be white for very long. A long
family-style table took up a section of the dancing area, forcing
people to be backed into the corner. Some candles flickered as the
bar became dimly lit. There was
an old upright piano against the

wall, with books on it and some ivy scaling up the wall to the ceiling. This place was a whole vibe, as the kids say.

As the DJ got going into his set, the music bounced between Janet Jackson, TLC, Missy Elliot, and some older 90s jams.

The atmosphere was perfect with heavy summer heat and the desire to be close with someone. You knew that you were going to sweat because the air in the room was thick. My hair started to curl and I swayed my hips feeling the music. I felt free to move and be myself.

And it happened. Sipping and talking to my gal pals, we decided it was time to start dancing. From across the room, I saw HIM. I quickly poured back the last of my drink and locked in on HIM. Yes ladies, it was that movie moment for me. I wanted to be close and dance with HIM. I could have taken my pointer finger or a yardstick, just about anything to direct a beam of light shooting out of my eyes. Straight across the bar, through the dark, I wanted to be right next to HIM.

It's so hard to explain, but maybe let me put it this way. Have you ever been out on a Sunday night to a Trader Joe's grocery store—you're standing in front of the frozen food section—and look over and see HIM at the end of the aisle? You just want to reach for the same frozen cauliflower crust pizza so you can talk to HIM?! Or maybe it is the wine section or granola boxes. Never have you ever seen HIM before but Lord Almighty you make note of the time and promise yourself you will be back every week 'til you get to talk with HIM.

I had a smile on my face because standing in that bar with a drink in hand, I didn't know how or when or what was going to happen, but I really hoped that this guy saw me. The confidence I had inside was shining on the outside. There was this electricity flowing out of me and surely it was going to electrify him with my confident smile.

HE was with some friends that were quite a bit taller. They appeared to be athletic, kind in the eyes, and goofy in shaking their shoulders from side to side. Their body language revealed to me that they didn't know what they were doing, but were ready to enjoy the night ahead.

I could tell HE was younger, for his light brown hair was parted down in the middle like Jonathan Taylor Thomas. He was sporting some cotton gray shorts, a light melon colored T-shirt, and rocking some low-cut Vans. Perfect. A+ for my kind of style. I remember thinking that we would look good together.

My two girlfriends and I, after taking a few laps around the room, did find our way to the dance floor. I was keeping an eye on HIM, as he walked to the bar to grab a drink with his friends. All of a sudden three guys in plaid button-up shirts were talking to us ladies. I could barely hear what they were saying above the music. I was not interested in what they were going to say so I turned my back and ignored them.

These blue and white check variety guys with their beer glasses seemed very confident as they approached my friends and me, and immediately started oversharing everything from why they were in town to how they found this bar. Apparently, in their quick Google search, this was the spot for dancing and they wanted to know when it was all going to really get started. Um, well, ya gotta dance, dudes. After all the get-to-know-you questions, I had to exit. We didn't need to get involved with these guys, so I pulled my friends away. No need to entertain men who were drinking real fast to unbutton a few from their collars.

With the room getting even louder, people were dancing and drinks were spilling as the floor got a little sticky. My girlfriends and I had found our groove, keeping to ourselves in a small corner. Moving our bodies from side to side, rocking hips and heads going back, with hands in the air, we were having a good time. My body felt so alive and filled with excitement. The time was going to be limited because I had driven and I knew my girlfriends didn't want to stay out late. We had to make the most out of this night. My drink was giving me a little buzz.

Feeling like hours had passed, I spotted HIM from earlier. He was coming out on the dance floor next to his friends who were standing cautiously in the corner.

Drink in hand, HE starts to dance as I did that thing you do—where you look over your shoulder, laughing with your girlfriends, just chuckling to let HIM know that I was care-free and fun. Putting my arms in the air because there is no space for them below, I do what any easy breezy girl shouldn't do. As I spun myself around, I brought my arms down from the sky. In one perfect swoosh, I knocked HIS drink out of his hands. CRASH—my elbow lands in his glass, beer is flying over onto the floor, as he jumps back hold-ing the drink away from his body. What a meet-cute?!! We caught eyes, leaning in and saying "I am so sorry!!" He shakes his head, "Nah it's okay." "Can I buy you another drink? I feel so bad!" He shakes his head again, tossing back the last few drops in the glass. Leaning in closer this time, touching his right shoulder, smiling a little, "Hi. I am Abbie." "My name is Brian."

Let the night officially begin! I was talking to HIM! Acciden-tally knocking this guy's drink was not how I planned on getting his attention, but there we were. From that moment on, we were locked together. I could've danced with him for hours. Something about the energy in the room and connecting with him made my heart smile. I let myself enjoy these moments, disregarding any previous notions I had about dancing with men I had just met.

As if we were characters playing out a scene in a PG-13 rom-com movie, I didn't want to have unrealistic expectations that this guy was going to be my "forever." But damn, it felt good to be dancing with someone. Side-by-side, moving back and forth, our bodies were in sync.

His hands would slide down my inner thighs and it was intox-icating to catch a breath with someone dancing from behind. The room temperature kept getting hotter as the sexual tension was rising. I felt safe and was having a good time. I ended up meeting Brian's guy friends while completely forgetting about who I came with. They were all soccer players at a university and had come to Portland for a night out.

Back and forth, round and round, moving to whatever the DJ was throwing down, Brian and I made a night of it. His hands would slowly find their way along the contour of my body, shooting electricity from my head to my toes. I wanted more but I was dripping in sweat. As we danced, pools of hot summer were forming in my bra, lower back, and hips.

Sharing the same space, super close and touching one another, I reached towards him, taking his shirt and pulling it towards me. I wiped my sweaty face on HIS T-shirt. We were basically sweating on each other already, right? My mint crop top was so tight that if I would have tried to use my own shirt, my bra would have been out for all to see. Now my sweat was embedded into the fibers of his melon shirt. I stepped back and immediately regretted reaching for his shirt. *Did he think I was weird for using his shirt as a towel? Had I just done something completely disgusting? Was he going to want to keep dancing with me?* I continued to linger in the moment, wondering if other girls have done the same thing.

This stuck with me for a while, I think because I felt embarrassed to reach for something that wasn't mine. I didn't know this guy and figured I missed the memo on dance floor code of conduct. But, I didn't have time to ask or see if my sweat-wiping had any consequences on the night. Before I knew it, my girlfriends were pulling me to go.

Looking back on this night, all I wanted was to be connected to someone. Finding myself on the dance floor that night opened my eyes to inner freedom that I was seeking. To be given the opportunity to embrace attraction with someone, enjoy it freely, and remember that I can be physically close to someone. I was rewriting the narrative that good girls keep their hands to themselves, by allowing myself to have chemistry with a stranger. You are allowed to have fun when going out. Give yourself permission to embrace a connection with someone; it feels so good to be confident in your own skin. As I embraced the moment, I found joy that was empowering. Get out on the dance floor. Go reach for those T-shirts.

FEELING GOOD LIKE I SHOULD

CHECK IN ON YOURSELF

Sketch a person whom you are attracted to. Maybe even someone you'd love to meet. If drawing's not your thing, trace their face from your cell phone screen.

CHAPTER 11

Posting for the Likes

Waking up, I pulled the blue comforter with multiple covers back from my chest, swinging my knees over the side of the bed. Rolling my neck and stretching my arms, I gave a little pause before I wiped my eyes and hopped down onto the floor. I sensed a cloud was hanging over me. The day had just started but already I wasn't feeling it. A few things contributed to this uneasy feeling. I hadn't gotten enough sleep the previous nights, and some serious looming deadlines were on my calendar. My mind went directly to the laundry list of tasks to get done. I quickly became overwhelmed with everything to do. *How can I do it all?* The emphasis was not wanting to let me or anybody down. Stuff needed to get done! I spiraled into a *I am not doing enough* frame of mind. It was a battle to remind myself that I needed to show up and do my best, but my validation and worth does not come from the work I produce. I needed to draw out what was already inside of me. I sensed that I needed an extra boost for the day. I needed some breakfast, but first I had to change my clothes.

Looking in my closet, I found an outfit I hadn't worn in a while. A black romper with its sweetheart cut top, mesh sleeves, pockets, and shorts which allow for my legs to extend out, it felt like the right choice. I slipped my feet into a pair of tall chunky black boots that elevated my mood along with my height. I didn't feel that energetic and found myself in a bit of a fog, so my favorite platform boots had to add a little fun to my step.

With a full day of work ahead of me, I had to do something just for me, even for just five minutes. I needed to be kind and give myself grace so that the day was not completely lost by the feelings that bogged me down. I knew that if I took care of myself on the outside, then it would help me feel better on the inside. This in turn would likely help me get more done. A mental shift was slowly being made as I glanced at myself quickly in my bedroom mirror. I decided to speak a truth over myself—"you are so beautiful"—and head to my bathroom to wash my face. While in the bathroom I noticed a framed piece of art that read, "we think you are really pretty." I repeated these self-affirmations over and over.

Giving myself a smile, I noticed an inner confidence surfacing. This outfit was just an outfit, but I felt more alive after putting it on, shining outward. Reaching for a big-brimmed black hat with leather cord, I made my way into my living room. Sunbeams came through the window into my space, lighting up the whole room as I approached my full-length mirror. I chose to show up for the day with love for myself. No matter if I woke up on the wrong side of the bed, it was my inner joy that slowly resurfaced.

With the lighting perfect in my living room, I extended my left foot out in front of my right foot. I turned my hips towards the mirror, twisting just a little. Holding my camera in my left hand, I angled the lens down to capture my best side. SNAP—I took a picture of myself, not looking directly ahead but just looking down. I contemplated posting the photo right away to Instagram but decided to put my phone aside, and placed it on the couch. As I stepped away from the mirror I slid my hands into my romper pockets, spinning around a few times, taking notice of how I was feeling. *Okay girl you get after this day. Everything is working out for your good.* Turning on some favorite songs, I ended up dancing around my living room for ten minutes. I embraced the day with a renewed sense of excitement.

After I had some breakfast, I returned to my phone. Grabbing the device in my right hand, I tapped on the front screen, smiling at my background picture. It was of my sister and me laughing, taken a few years ago. I see the picture every day on my phone, but this time felt important. Without her even knowing it, she was encouraging me and uplifting me with her smile.

Shaking off the dissatisfaction I felt earlier, I reframed my thoughts about myself and reminded myself of what was going to make me come alive today. I decided I would share my photo online. Getting some likes and validation from my friends would be the icing on the cake to my turned-around morning. With a bounce in my step, I gave myself permission to rewrite the day.

Years ago, if I posted a selfie like this, it was because I desired a quick fix of self-affirmation and only got shallow validation. It didn't matter the number of likes or hearts coming in. Constantly desiring a dopamine hit, I would be glued to my phone for hours, refreshing, trying to believe that the comments coming in were real and that the rush of the attention would last. I wanted a self-esteem boost from something external, with motivation steeped in "this will make me feel better." If people told me I was looking good, then I should feel good. I was annoyed with myself for being so needy but I didn't know how to stop. Posting to my stories became semi-addictive. But thank you, Mark Zuckerberg, for wanting us all to be obsessed with your platform.

Now I know I have immeasurable worth, and posting a selfie like this comes from a place of wanting to share my life with no expectations. There is a deep respect for the inner work I have done on myself and no longer seeking full approval from others. I believe that what makes me beautiful is how my flaws are knit together with my beating heart, and this has nothing to do with putting on a stellar outfit. Outwardly I am living in the confidence of who I am becoming on the inside. All the smiley faces, red hearts, and thumbs-up emoji comments are secondary to the inner confidence and validation coming first from within.

There is nothing wrong with wanting to share and show off a bit, believing that in our skin we have this brilliance. It just gets down to intention. We are made of brave, bold brilliance and we can shine. We can shine at home by ourselves and we can shine when we post a picture. We can shine even when we don't have the words to say or the outfit to put on. By showing up and being present for ourselves day in and day out, there are opportunities that allow us to truly shine. No more ulterior motives, only poppin' our best foot forward.

NO FILTER
NEEDED

CHECK IN ON YOURSELF

Find two pictures of yourself: one favorite, one not-so-favorite. Option to print and paste or just describe. Reflect on what separates the two pictures in your mind.

favorite picture
of yourself
↓

not so favorite
picture of
yourself
↓

CHAPTER 12

That One Time I Tried Yoga

Looking around the studio, I hoped to see someone else struggling through a sun salutation. The instructor told me I'm doing fine and brought me all the blocks. Non-Groupon yogis gave me side-eyes. I knew my movements were distracting. Or was it my heavy breathing?

I had just moved to Portland, Oregon, to live with my dearest friend Whitney. She was kind enough to let me stay with her in a small condo just off of Northwest 21st and Irving. This was a very trendy part of Portlandia. A few months prior, I graduated with my Master of Fine Arts degree and was on the search for a job. With a wide open schedule, I searched for things to do and ways to meet new people. One evening getting ready for bed, we were brushing our teeth. She looked over at me and said, "Hey, want to do some yoga classes with me? There is a Groupon for a studio really close to here. We could go together."

I told her yes as I spit out my toothpaste in the sink. I heard that everybody in Portland did yoga, so what better way to connect with people than to take some classes? I mentioned to

Whitney I had never done yoga before, but she said the class punch card would be perfect. I could try it out and learn right alongside others. If I ended up loving it, I could purchase more sessions. It was low risk and an easy yes for me.

Because she worked a full-time job, we planned to attend the morning class. But we are talking SUPER early—6 a.m. My living arrangement was situated in the living room on one of those roll-away beds, and during the day it was tucked under a shelving unit. Sometimes I pretended I was on a ship, as the wheels sort of rolled when I moved from my back to my side while laying down. I cautiously leaned over the right side, sitting up to put on my workout attire. It was early morning and I had a hard time locating my shoes. Even though I was super tired, I was excited to try this new activity. Picking up my fresh gray yoga mat and a bottle of water, Whitney drove us over to the studio. We could have walked but it was just too far for such an early morning. I was glad we were doing this together and hoped the instructor would kindly guide me throughout the class.

Finding a parking spot, we flung our bodies out of the car and dashed into the front room of this tiny building. Nobody talked as they waited for the doors to open. Some light music was playing, and all the lights were low. This all amounted to setting a calm mood. I shoved my stuff into a little cubby and noticed people had their shoes off. Untying mine, I threw those aside too. I realized there was nothing calm about my actions, so I gently took my water bottle out of my backpack and took a sip. I kept looking around, trying to act cool, wanting people to not pick up on the fact that I was a first-timer. *Uffda,* it was already warm in the waiting room.

My thoughts raced a bit as the instructor opened the classroom door and we all made our way to a spot throughout the room. The class was good for beginners but all levels were welcome to attend. *Was I going to be able to move like other people? What if I got dizzy having my head upside down? Would there be music playing during class? Where do I go if I need to use the bathroom? Was I wearing the right kind of clothes?* I noticed myself becoming all too aware of my surroundings and felt a bit out of place. I was an artist after all, but maybe I could become more athletic. Looking over at Whitney, she smiled back at me. This wasn't her first time, but I could tell this was right in line with her natural abilities either way. She told me I would love these exercises and stretches. What better way to get more connected to my body and with others than to start with yoga?

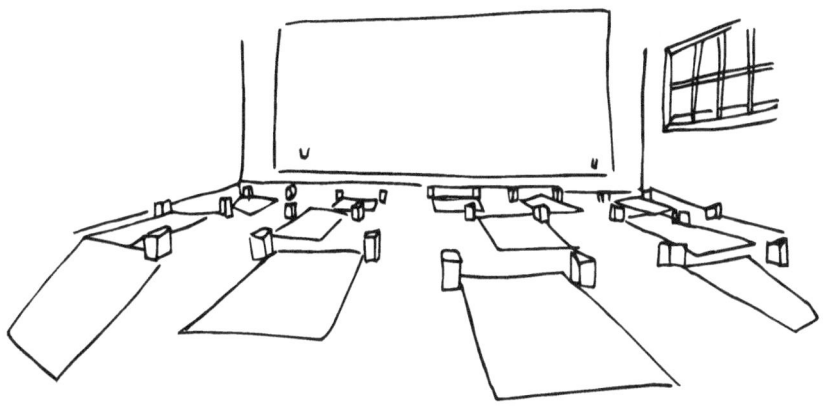

I thought being barefoot was kind of disgusting as I found a place to throw down my mat. I picked this gray thing up from Target for ten bucks the day before. Always getting those good deals, am I right? The room was dimly lit, shades were all pulled down across the wall of windows, and a floor-to-ceiling mirror went across the front of this small room. I noticed the warm temperature as more people filed in. Outfits were loose or tight fitting, with colors that were muted and soft. I was wearing a band T-shirt with cheap Target black leggings. Some nervousness started to surface as I tried to stretch like the pro yogis in front of me.

Nobody had started yet and it was already warm. News flash, this wasn't hot yoga!! I was going to be in trouble. *Would I have sweat marks on my butt as I put a leg in the air? What if my hands got sweaty and made my mat slick? Was I going to be able to breathe with my asthma?*

Yoga for all levels, they said. Probably was for the best since I didn't even know the various kinds and varieties. As we started the class, I noticed very quickly that my body was wobbly. Maybe this was because I hadn't had breakfast or because the poses were so foreign to my body. I had never done yoga before those first few classes—did I mention that?

The instructor guided us through different stretches giving us voice prompts about how to move our bodies, where to place our hands and legs, and telling us how to use our breath. As the room filled with heavy breathing, I didn't know how to join in. The inhales, exhales, grunts, and sighs all sounded so labored, as if Serena Williams was in the room. And between my body being super contoured trying to get these poses down, I started to chuckle at myself. I had half expected to be decent at yoga because I had seen people do it on YouTube and out at parks. Everyone moved with ease and confidence. I was a wet noodle with tight hips and bad wrists. I just wanted to look like the others in the room and I didn't. Not even close.

Coming from a choral background, I knew how to let my chest lift and fall. The breathing part was the only thing that came naturally.

I was trying really hard to keep it together, as my body was forming different movements and iterations that it had never been in before. At one point, the instructor came over and let me know that because my knees could not touch the ground when I sat cross-legged, it was OK to use the blocks to keep myself propped up. Y'all, I didn't just have one block. She stacked me up with four. If I felt embarrassed walking in the door, I really felt it now. When I get nervous, I start laughing. I was trying not to take myself too seriously because I didn't want to be anxious in a class that was meant to be calming to my nervous system.

The goal for the next pose was to be bent over, feet crossed over knees. The way that my hips were positioned automatically sent me falling backward. It was inevitable. The blocks underneath both knees did not help at all. Looking around the room, I felt eyes on me. Ambient music played, and sweat dripped down my neck and pooled in my lower back. I lost all concentration. The mood was set to relax and I was anything but relaxed. My body was falling over. As the instructor made her way around the room, she mentioned that no matter how you showed up to class, your skill level or your physical makeup, we all were in this together. It made me feel a little better that I was using all those blocks when everyone else wasn't. Many people in that room were seasoned yogis and I know they thought I looked ridiculous. I was sitting there, trying to prop myself up and using good posture. But I kept falling over.

I was wobbly and wonky. Shit, and I think I pulled a muscle in my right thigh. My body was being realigned by the instructor every single pose. She fixed my arm from being in the wrong direction, readjusted my legs, and gave me alternatives for my bad wrists. Whitney on the other hand was a graceful swan, extending limbs with lightness and poise. With every flow, she could anticipate what was coming next as if she'd been to this class hundreds of times before.

As I got through the class, I kept getting this feeling that I wanted to fit in and wanted to be a part of something. Being new to Portland, and knowing lots of locals do yoga, I desired to share in this activity. If others were finding friendship in going to classes, I wanted to be good at it to make friends. In trying something new, I knew there was a chance I might need to keep going back to practice so I could get better at the exercises. I had a fear that people weren't going to like the wobbly girl if they saw me again. I didn't want to be a distraction for others, but I wanted to be a part of this.

Over the course of the ten classes, because Whitney and I did finish our Groupon punch pass, I got more and more comfortable with my body's own discomfort. With my friend's accountability and encouragement, I was able to see past the perfectionism and feelings of needing to fit in. I could show up with my wonky awkward body and keep trying. I had this deep desire to accept myself and feel like I was making a difference in my body. The improvement came as I showed up, dropped the "I can'ts," and the instructor guided us through each class. I had to ignore the lie that said I would never be good at this activity. I learned that although I had some tight hip genes passed down from my mother, I too could stand and do a warrior pose like a pro.

I gave myself more patience in my last few classes, not concerning myself with what others thought of my body placement, positions, and need for props. Being present with myself, I realized I didn't have to look a certain way or be a certain way, Lululemon or not. The internal work was about taking a pause, being mindful of my body, and allowing myself to take up space even if I was falling over.

We are allowed to be completely and utterly ourselves. Extend your limbs and put yourself out there. You are right where you need to be, even if you're propped up by blocks. Besides, nobody is really watching you as much as you think they are.

NOBODY IS
REALLY
WATCHING
YOU AS MUCH
AS YOU
THINK THEY
ARE

CHECK IN ON YOURSELF

Take five minutes to focus on your breathing. Inhale and exhale and notice your chest rising and falling. Write out your findings here.

_____

_____

_____

_____

_____

_____

_____

_____

_____

_____

_____

_____

_____

_____

_____

_____

_____

_____

_____

_____

_____

_____

_____

_____

_____

_____

_____

See page 213 for some breathing techniques.

CHAPTER 13

Say Hi to the Algorithm for Me. I'm Out.

Pre-recorded message:
    "We can't come to the phone right now, so please leave your name, number, and a brief message for Denise, Derek, Joe, Karlee, or Kim Johnson. We will get back to you as soon as we can!" Automated female voice:

"Please leave your message after the tone"….. BEEEEEEEP-PPP…

"Hey Kim, it's Abbie calling. Wanted to see if you would come outside and play. Maybe we could ride bikes around the cul-de-sac. My mom said it'd be fine. So. . . (long pause) Just call me back when you get this. Okay. . . (another long pause) BYE."

When I left my home on Harrow Avenue those summer afternoons, I was gone. My mom called me back to our house from my friend's place using a phone that worked even when the power went out. I grew up in the heyday of the landline and the answering machine. Communication was less frequent and less complicated. I was out more than I was home but somehow more present everywhere I went.

My sister, Allie, would often be down the street at her friend's house. I'd go in the other direction. When it was dinner time, we'd run home, wash our hands, and get ready for supper. If we were out during the day, we'd come home excited to check the machine. There was this sort of thrill and anxiousness about who may have called. Because this phone was connected to a landline, the machine was for the whole house. All messages were fair game for ANYONE to listen to. I remember being especially petrified if a boy I had a crush on left a message. With my parents, two older siblings, and my younger sister all receiving potential calls each day, the answering machine would often fill up. Yep—when someone wanted to leave a message, but the tape was full, you were out of luck. It was our job to delete any message we didn't need anymore. Sometimes a friend would leave multiple messages back to back because the recorder would cut them off. It was hilarious to have to piece together all the information.

Cordless phones changed things. But not a lot—nothing like how cell phones and texting would change the game. In college, I would have to wait until I was near the dorm phone or meet in person to talk to my boyfriend; there was no walking through campus while having conversations at my fingertips.

Once, I talked to him for eight hours uninterrupted until the battery beeped and I had to say goodbye. There was this magic in talking like that, allowing it to go on and on, so seamlessly, no FaceTime, no plans to meet up. And there was magic in the messages I saved on my answering machines for years, even though it left a little less space for other callers.

Cell phones changed things. A lot.

They brought about an immediacy—to everything. I would like to say this is a good thing, but it stresses me out. I feel the need to answer every call exactly when it comes in. *What is good phone etiquette? Is it rude not to pick up right away? Do I have to call back right away? Do people even listen to voicemails when we can just text?*

Today, I wanted to get a chai tea down the street. I was only going to be gone for 15 minutes.

Got keys? Yep. Wallet? Check. Cell phone? Che…..Nope. Don't need it. Leaving that behind on purpose. In order to not forget anything, I went through a mental checklist.

Hopping down the street carefree, I was pumped to get my beverage. Ain't no thang to leave the phone behind. Two seconds out the door, I saw some beautiful flowers. I reached for my phone in my pocket. Oh yeah, not there. Five seconds away from my door, crossing the street, I decided I should call my mom. No can do. No phone. My brain was having a mind fart, trained to check my pockets every other second. To scroll or not to scroll, my fingers have a mind of their own. I tried to fight the urge.

While almost to Stumptown Coffee, I ran into my friend Jen. She yelled at me from across the street as she walked towards me.

"Hey Abbie, What's up? Want to run errands with me?"

I tell you, this was not planned. Repeat. This was not planned. Could this kind of stuff even happen in the 2020s?

I didn't know what I would be getting into, but I knew Jen makes everything fun. Her smile. Her jokes. Her goofy, funny stories and banter. I got my chai, and with it in hand, I slid into the passenger seat of her friend's small pickup. Jen is tall and her head grazed the top of the ceiling. We stayed in park for a moment as she told me how her day was going. She wanted cookies, and needed to grab food from a kitchen she volunteers at, and then drop it off 20 minutes away.

We laughed and talked and let the rain come in the windows. We used her phone like an old-school Walkman, playing music in the background. She didn't have a data plan on the phone, so there weren't any notifications coming in. With no possible distractions, we just plugged it into the speakers. Such a perfect date — I couldn't have planned it if I tried.

And if I'd had my cell phone?

Outside my door, I'd have taken my classic feet-with-flowers photo, mostly for myself, to remember the beauty of the moment, maybe to post. I would have booked it to the cafe, sharing my tea with a photo and a tag in my stories, letting people know I left the house and supported a local spot. I definitely would have video-recorded Jen singing along to her playlist's top 20 songs and hashtagged the shit out of it: #dontstop #ladiesunite #bestdayever. Jen was being hands and feet in the community, volunteering at a local non-profit, taking time out of her schedule to deliver meals to those in need. All my followers needed to view that.

But honestly? If I'd had my phone that morning, I might have missed seeing Jen. I might have been looking down at the moment she passed by—both of us unknowingly missing an opportunity. I got to see and know my friend better because I wasn't thinking about likes and hashtags. I was freed to feel the presence of a real human and her joyful beauty right next to me in real time.

And guess what? When I returned home: no new calls, no voicemail. Nothing had changed. Usually, when I want to leave my phone behind, I'm plagued with thoughts of:

WHAT IF SOMEONE NEEDS TO REACH ME?

WHAT IF SOMEONE NEEDS TO GET AHOLD OF ME?

WHAT IF I WANT TO TAKE A SELFIE WITH MY SMOOTHIE OR SNEAK A PIC OF MY HANDS HOLDING A NEW SCRUNCHIE ON SALE AT TARGET?

WHAT IF THERE WAS A DEAL I NEEDED TO TELL MY BESTIE ABOUT?

WHAT IF I MISS A BOOMERANG MOMENT?

WHAT IF I DON'T DOCUMENT EVERYTHING?

As if the world needs to see my play-by-play.

Maybe that's the point folks make when they say there is beauty in experiencing our world without distractions. Our experiences will not all get documented because they are not meant to be.

Not going to lie, when I slipped into the truck with Jen, I panicked a bit about not having my phone. Nobody knew where I was going if they needed me. But what if I just needed some space to be? To have a good time with a lovely human and not consumed by a spiral of advertisements and celebrity couples?

Let's get back to the days of our youth. For me, yes, that is referencing the late 80s and early 90s when a cell phone was only used by dreamy Zac Morris. Being in touch with people and staying connected is, in and of itself, a really good thing. But so is a pause. An afternoon where we are just with ourselves and those around—in person, not virtually.

Give your phone a little "do not disturb" switch, take off your Apple Watch, leave the AirPods out. Get outside and take a short walk without it all. Maybe randomly visit a friend's house unannounced to see if they want to take a quick bike ride. Write down your grocery list on paper and swing by the store. Notice what feelings are stirred up. Do you embrace the moment? Does anxiety, fear, or a wandering mind come to play? Do you answer every single call, or let the answering machine store whatever it has room for?

LET IT
GO TO
VOICEMAIL

CHECK IN ON YOURSELF

Power off your phone for a couple of hours and head out on an algorithm-free adventure. Write about what you did, noticed, and felt during this time afterward.

CHAPTER 14

Framing the Sky

Whenever I visit my sister in Minneapolis, Minnesota, we go to the Walker Art Center. I insist that we go every time and I tell her it's like seeing our old friends. We have to check in on them and say hello. What I love about this museum, specifically, is that it has a sculpture garden connected to it.

My first experience going to the sculpture garden was on a date with a guy named Matt. He wanted to show me some things and we toured the whole gallery. He asked me to follow him outside. "I want to take you to one of my favorite places."

We walked up some very steep stone steps to a flowing path that was green. Grasses and other sculptures were close by. He then led me to a wide-angled tunnel partially underground where you feel like you are going into the earth. As we walked through this cemented carved path, it opened up to a beautiful outdoor room. There was only a half ceiling due to a large cut-out square overhead. This opening allowed us to look up and see directly through to the sky. Not a fully enclosed ceiling like most rooms—this one was open. We sat down on these very large flat slate benches, which reached up over 10 feet tall toward the ceiling and encircled the whole room. They were cool to the touch but the air coming in was warm. The walls of this space were white just above the slate where the walls meet. There was no physical door, but an opening to walk through.

Walking into this art piece that opened up the sky above, framing the sky, I felt like I could reach out and grab the clouds. Many birds would fly in and perch at the top of the slate ledge near the ceiling and then freely rush back out again. When looking up everything overhead, a plane, bugs, pollen, and leaves could fall down landing in your lap. Laying my body down across the seated area and resting my head down, I spread out on this bench. I gazed my eyes up at the sky.

Blue clouds were moving by in all of their whimsy and personality. With my head still resting on the bench, I felt like I was in a movie that was simultaneously playing out before my eyes. Matt was next to me sitting cross-legged. Resting my arms behind my head, I was left in a trance. I didn't want to move.

Mesmerized by this moving picture, time slowed down and everything was still, quiet, at rest.

Sometimes it feels like my life is passing me by, going from one existential crisis to the next. I'm always wondering if I am wasting my days. *Is what I am doing worthwhile? Does my life have purpose and meaning? Am I going to matter to someone? What am I doing here?*

But I was, in that moment, present, and there was a depth and a richness in the color. I noticed the color blue, I noticed the brilliance of the "out there." It was almost as if I could pick up my paintbrush and paint in a scene. I've done a few time-lapse videos of it and it's like the clouds move through so intentionally. Each cloud is seemingly given a name with a story to tell of all their travels.

I found my body sitting on a stone in a box looking out at the world beyond this box again, this time, with my sister. I think because of the way we were designed, we need this kind of space for reflection. An invitation to be known not by anyone else, but to ourselves. Allowing our thoughts to settle in a blue color.

Even a gray sky will look and have a tint of blue in there because of the way the light casts a shadow depending on the time of day. The sun rotates and navigates around the earth and you get this different shadow cast. There's no roof in this earth cave.

If it's raining, the rain comes, and if it's snowing, the snow comes in, and if it's windy, the wind will come in and swirl around on the inside.

There are crickets that find their way in and plop right next to you and chirp away and sometimes startle you. There are birds that make their way inside and their chirps bounce around the walls. There's an echo in there that sound the acoustics of human footsteps coming in and going out—giving a warning to those sitting inside.

I could sit in there for hours. There's something about the pressure of the air. I look up at the sky and have a great sense of wonder. *What does today hold and what will tomorrow bring? How do I reach out from the here and now, into the heavens and let it fall as it will?* Maybe there are not enough moments or times when we can lay on our backs, extend our hands to the sky and be in gratitude.

We need more time to exist, being and doing nothing more than listening in. We can feel alive. It's not magical really, but when I sit in that space, I know that I'm becoming more aware of the great "out there." Somehow, right here and right now, time passes. The artist gives context to make room for a world full of endless possibilities. The sun—she rises and she sets.

THE LIGHT
IT TOUCHES
EACH ONE
OF US

CHECK IN ON YOURSELF

Fill in the Sky Pesher illustration with a short list of places and spaces where you feel wonder.

_____

_____

_____

_____

_____

_____

_____

_____

_____

_____

_____

_____

_____

_____

_____

_____

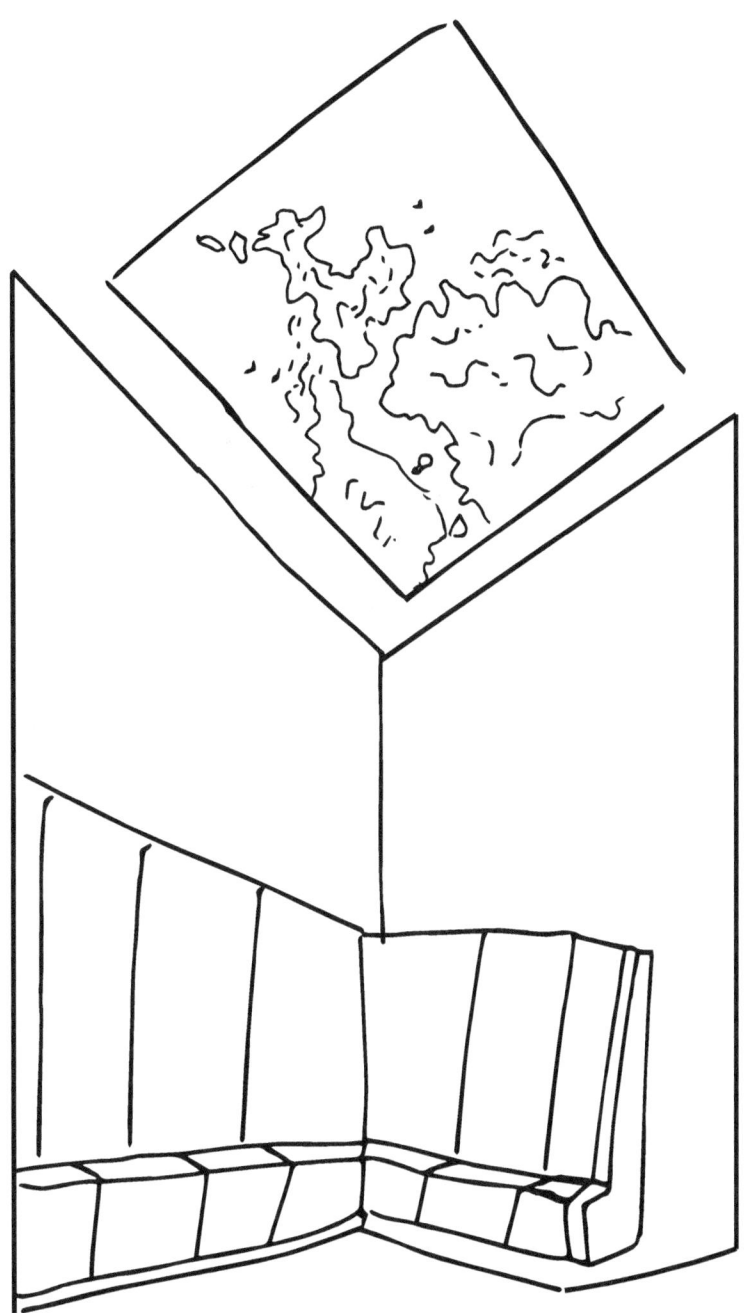

CHAPTER 15

Nobody Standing Still

The Wonder Ballroom. A perfect location for a smaller, more intimate setting. Not for ballroom dancing but to see your favorite indie bands live. This place holds many special memories as music has a way of bringing people together. I have spent lots of nights swaying hips, harmonizing at the top of my lungs with complete strangers, feet tired from standing on concrete for hours. No matter who was playing, the shows were always lively and entertaining, well worth the ticket price.

Live music had just come back, or at least bands were safely touring again, since the pandemic shut much of the country down. Portland was shut down for longer than most parts of the country. So long, in fact, that my favorite acts hadn't been able to play in my city due to restrictions and mandates. It was totally fine, I understood why. But it was hard to not be dancing to my favorite tunes in a live show setting.

I was having an off day and decided to look up the music I listened to on my phone. I noticed an album from a band in Australia—*Middle Kids*. Because of the burn to see a live show that was itching within me, I just googled their name and clicked on "shows." OH MY GOODNESS I found that they were playing my city THAT NIGHT—that exact night. I quickly bought my tickets.

Did you have an album or two that carried you through the pandemic? Something that you put on to soothe the weeks? This was the band for me.

The venue they played at required you to show proof of vaccination or a negative rapid test upon arrival. It was a small price to pay after not hearing live music for two years—not to mention music by the band that got me through the pandemic.

The room was dark, the crowd was sparse, and masks came off and back on with every sip of beer. The folks slowly kept coming in. As they did, the people next to me got closer and closer. I was at the show alone, casually by myself, which was something I frequently did. I was trying to keep my phone in my pocket instead of "checking emails and sending messages or scrolling Instagram." I wanted to be present for this moment—a live music show. It had been over a year and a half since I was at a concert coming out of the pandemic times. Being around so many people indoors almost felt like I was doing something wrong.

The opening band played and they were quite fun. They used an old spiral cord telephone to distort their voices into the microphone. They called their style "electric elevator music." Their show fit the vibe they were going for. I imagined I was in a building, walking into an elevator, rising up many floors, to then be taken back down. The anticipation for the main act rose as we were ready and warmed up to hear our favorite songs.

The headlining band had flown in from their latest city, originally from Australia, and were extremely fired up to be in the room. As soon as they hit the stage, the lead singer went into a whole swearing excitement statement, explaining how thrilled they were to be sharing their music with us. She jumped up and down, firing up her guitar, letting out some riffs and chords, continuing to talk about what it meant to the band that we had all shown up to hear them. She wanted us to know that being in front of a real live audience, people standing before them, was a complete rush. The crowd cheered and raised their beverages of choice, each smiling and taking in the moment.

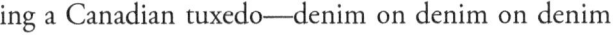

There were two gentlemen ahead of me to the left, who were very enthusiastic. One had a mullet and the other had bleached hair wearing a Canadian tuxedo—denim on denim on denim. The other had on a white tank top, a loose floral button-up not buttoned, and Vans. They seemed to be really into each other and as they cheered drinks together, they smiled. One put their arm around the other at the end of the song. I was surrounded by quirky dance moves, expressing and embracing the melody. It was like nobody else was in the room. Being together never felt so right!

In a room full of strangers, we couldn't help but feel connected. When the first notes hit the guitar and drums came in, it was as if a secret code in the room had been cracked open and nobody was standing still.

One song entitled "R U For Me" started, and as the song continued on the melody broke off with the singer yelling "Ha Ha." It cut to an instrumental section in which all the band went nuts. The whole room let loose; the joy was contagious. Music has a way of doing this—it can send you into a different dimension.

As the night progressed, we all seemed to get more comfortable around each other—the closest we had been in years. Being aware of the space around me, I kept my movements small at first, but watching the gentlemen ahead of me, I started to step out of my comfort zone. It didn't matter that I had shown up by myself; I was a part of a collective now. Seeing different people around me experience the music in their own way brought us all back to life. I wanted that, and more of it. The music was electrifying our bones, and sharing this moment was something so beautiful. Going to a live show after a year and a half of nothing—no music, no sharing space—and sweating close to one another—it was wild to be in the room. Electric. They band continued to perform their guts out. WOW. Incredible. The energy coming from the musicians caused the lead singer to start to cry. A sweet release as I started to tear up, too.

Shaking my hips and swaying my legs, noticing all the smiles on people's faces around the room, caused an infectious, joyful feeling to float through the air. I know I felt a little hesitant to go to a show by myself, stepping out of my comfort zone. But live music was back. In came a rush I had missed over the past year. The amount of time I had spent cooped up in my apartment compared to the collective energy in that room felt monumental. Tears welled up in my eyes that made me want to hug random people next to me. I finally didn't feel like an island. I had made it out into the world safely, maneuvering this new normal. The emotions were intoxicating and welled up from inside my chest. I couldn't peel off the big ol' smile from my face. Even though the lights weren't bright within the space, the light coming from each person shone through. No matter what, we were all back together again being the light, spreading the light.

YOUR LIGHT
SHINES
THROUGH,
TOGETHER

CHECK IN ON YOURSELF

Grab a friend and go out for a walk, out dancing, or for a hike. Write out how these experiences make you feel.

_____

_____

_____

_____

_____

_____

_____

_____

_____

_____

_____

_____

_____

_____

_____

_____

_____

_____

CHAPTER 16

Ain't No Mountain High Enough

Just last summer I signed myself up for a trip of a lifetime with a company called The Ivy Brand. Drum roll please…I headed to Alaska for the first time on a backpacking adventure. I found this company while researching online, and learned that they specialized in one-of-a-kind trips, taking people all over the world to experience new places, building community, and fostering a sense of belonging. As I read about Ivy on their website, I felt like I aligned with their core values and all of the trip pictures looked like people were having a blast. Knowing I am an extroverted person, I thought being with strangers for a little over a week sounded fun. Why not?! YOLO.

Because I had never done this type of adventure before, I needed to up my gear game. I went on the search for a backpackers bag and quickly found a friend who graciously let me borrow hers. Next up were some hiking shoes. Thank you, REI, for having some good sales right before I left.

Looking over the itinerary, there were going to be lots of exciting things happening. Backpack camping up to a lake, kayaking through glacial waters, and ATVing through some mountain passes with loads of hiking, sightseeing, and good meals in between.

I didn't know anybody on the trip, but knew I would walk away with lifelong friendships.

During a pre-trip Zoom call, I met our leader, Sarah, and her husband, Scott. Both had been to Alaska before and shared their excitement for all the activities ahead. I learned I was the only person from the Pacific Northwest, while others would be flying to Alaska from North Carolina, Florida, Illinois, and Minnesota. Everyone seemed super kind and I could already tell I was going to love adventuring with this company.

My friends at home know me as Abigail the artist, not Abigail the athlete. I played basketball for a few years in junior high, and did some indoor bouldering at a rock gym in college, but beyond that I am not athletic. There are no hurt feelings about this fact, but I didn't like how stereotypes labeled artsy kids as "not being good at anything else." I always wondered if I could flip the narrative and surprise people by all of a sudden becoming a professional ping pong player. But let's be real, that's actually my sister Allie's thing.

At our pre-trip meeting, people asked questions about different things. I asked about my knees and my health since I have asthma. I expressed that I was nervous I would hold people back. Hiking was something a bunch of my friends do for fun but I never really had opportunities to go with them due to my work schedule. *What made me think now in my mid-thirties I could all of a sudden hike a mountain?* I worried that I wouldn't be able to keep up the pace. Being an asthmatic, I wondered if I would have to stop to take breaks so I could breathe properly. The reason I stopped pursuing basketball back in my youth was because running made me wheeze. *Was dancing twice a week building up my endurance enough? Should I be hiking at a higher elevation before I leave to build up my lung strength?* In the weeks before the trip, I started to get very anxious over the whole experience. I worried mostly about my bad knee not allowing me to reach the top, followed by did I have the right gear, and was I really going to be able to do all the things planned out in the itinerary?

Fast forward a few months later, and I found myself on a small flight to Seattle, then to Anchorage, Alaska. With my backpacker's bag slung over my right shoulder, orange floral bandana with blue and white striped Dickies denim overalls and tank top, high top Vans, and gold chain necklaces, I flexed my muscles in the bathroom mirror. I LOOKED like I could hike a mountain. I flashed a smile because I knew I was going to accomplish some amazing things on this trip that would stretch me both physically and mentally. *Let's go,* I thought. *You got this.*

Once in Alaska, I had to get on a smaller charter plane to Valdez. Grabbing a snack, I walked around the airport trying to locate where this lil' plane was taking off from. Led down a dingy hallway which felt like I was walking through a time warp with the 80s decorative style, I sat on a gray bench. Looking around the room at my fellow trippers, I thought, *Could any of these people be my new friends?* I became really excited waiting to board. The anticipation rose as the TSA worker called out that our flight was ready for us to get on the plane. We walked outside as the wind blew my curls right out. Strong weather was coming in but apparently it was still safe to fly. Once we all got situated into our seats, I was given a homemade cookie. Looking over to my right, I met my first new friend, Hannah. Because of how close the seats were together, I recognized her face from the Zoom call and we launched into making fun of each other right off the bat, quickly becoming best friends. Back and forth we cracked jokes as this little but mighty plane touched down in Valdez. Let the adventure begin! I was ready to conquer some fears and go after all this trip had for us.

First up, we stopped at a fish hatchery where we watched sea lions the size of small dinosaurs launch out of the water to grab their dinner. One of the guys on the trip ended up in the water, trying to fish for a salmon with his bare hands. The landscape of snow-capped mountains and glacial peaks looked like a painting, one that I wanted to reach out and touch. I couldn't believe the beauty I was taking in. The air was humid with a touch of salt. Stopping at The Fat Mermaid for our own salmon spread, my eyes opened wider than those sea lions. The group was getting to know one another over meals and I was definitely the jokester of the group. Later on, settling into our hotel, I found out I was rooming with Hannah. We unpacked our suitcases and immediately bounced onto our queen beds. With legs crossed and heads propped up on folded arms, we started sharing stories. It was shaping up to be the best adult slumber party.

The next day was filled with a smaller hike to get us prepared for our overnight backpacking excursion and kayaking through some glacial waters. I may or may not have sung some Disney movie songs as we paddled our way through incredible blue waters. Nothing like being your true authentic, funny self in a pristine natural setting. Everyone in the group got along really well and shared more than just our favorite colors. Alaska was shaping up to be everything I had hoped for and more than I could have dreamed.

A few days in, between snacking on gummy bears and granola bars, we were instructed to pack up our backpacking bags. The next night we were going to be hiking up a mountain with 50lbs on our backs. We would hike 4,000 feet in elevation gains to a lake. This mountain excursion was going to be challenging. At least for me. At least that is what I told myself. Various camping items went in our packs, from sleeping pads and sleeping bags, to utensils, camping chairs, tent parts, clothes, water bottles, etc. I made sure my Holga film camera with googly eyes made it in. *Could we see a bear on our hike? Was it going to rain on us? Would I get blisters on my heels from my boots?*

Still in the hotel room with Hannah, I suited up with my pack. Being completely silly, I went into full improv mode, making a video to send over to our leader Sarah in the next room. I get silly when I'm nervous. I squatted down and pretended to grab snacks, and did a fit check to see if I could reach out for some rocks. I even joked about spraying a bear away in my Birkenstock sandals. I don't think I was aware of how nervous I actually was. I let my guard down a little by being silly with Hannah, and her laughter helped. I recall telling her I had never hiked a mountain before and I was a little nervous. She told me her ACL was recovering so she had to wear a big brace. She assured me that we could take our time and climb up the mountain together.

I will never forget getting out of the fifteen passenger van, feet hitting the ground, dust flying around my hiking socks while I strapped up my Merrell boots. I wore all of my favorite things: a blue bandana, heart locket, black Blazers T-shirt, Nike leggings, and this bright blue Cotopaxi windbreaker with my tiger hat on. My hair was curly and cascading off the left and the right shoulders. My wrists were covered in friendship bracelets with the colorful chunky beads. This outfit was something I had been planning for weeks. I knew I wanted to "wear" into the hike as much confidence and badassery as I could.

I had my nails painted this periwinkle purple color. I slid my hands into the loops on the poles. I took out my albuterol inhaler, gave it two puffs, swished some water in my mouth and let my smile spread across my face. I knew I was about to do something that was going to cost me some of my fear. There was hope in coming back down, knowing I will have accomplished something great. I chose to show up for myself and be present. I allowed myself to be courageous enough to say, "I am going to try, I am going to go do it anyway." There was a shift in my mindset that no matter what, I could do great things—anything was possible.

We were off to locate the trailhead to Lower Reed Lake. The confidence I had earlier started to dip. The closer we got to actually getting on the trail, the more I gave my fears room to grow. The fear of not being able to reach the top took full root, starting in my head down to my toes. A small voice repeated the phrases *you are going to have trouble* and *how are you going to do this hike safely* and *fight that anxious urgency rising in your stomach*. Seeing off in the distance where we were going, it really dawned on me that I had never really hiked such elevation gains before. I freaked myself out.

We started walking on a gravel path that quickly became more rocky. As we got up higher, the air got thinner, the pack got heavier, my knees burned harder, and my confidence waned. I seriously should have done some stair stepper machines weeks ago. Wishing I had done more physical conditioning for this, I realized that I hadn't prepped my mind with the possibility that I was actually going to succeed. I felt both confident in my determination to complete what I set out to do, but quietly scared inside to get to the top. The negative self-talk had only been about not being able to keep up and keep going. But on the trail, I realized that I was doing it—I was a hiking gal. The only thing in my way was the mental block I had placed inside of me—telling myself I couldn't do it. I was breathing normally, my muscles were being worked so they would get tired, but my mind was getting reprogrammed. We passed more trees and went over bigger rocks and I still did it, I was hiking.

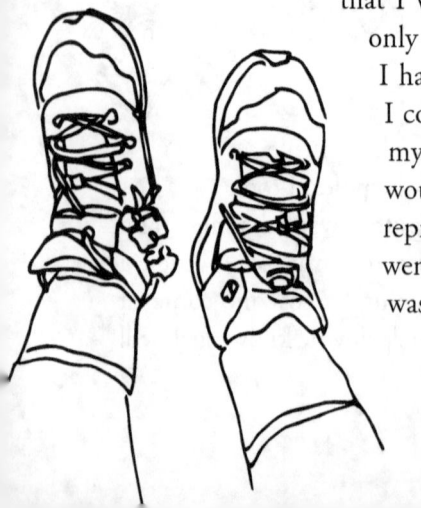

Having poles came in clutch for most

the way up, until without warning we came across a section of the mountain that had all oversized boulders. A smaller stream of water was rushing below the larger rocks. You could see it because the rocks piled on top of each other revealed beneath them various sections of the stream. I started fumbling around. I was used to bouldering in an indoor rock climbing gym, but not with a 50lb pack on. My bag started to swing a bit to the front, so I tightened the straps. I wished I could go back to the gradual inclines and winding paths lined with wildflowers.

Sarah had set the pace, and the brothers, Micah and Matthew, decided to go on up ahead. They were pumped to be on their own with walkie-talkies just in case they needed to be in touch.

Putting one foot in front of the other, exhausted and needing some assistance, I lunged myself forward. I started to slip and looked up, noticing nobody had their poles out any longer. A kind stranger helped me collapse mine down so I could put them into my bag. The group had made it across this section already and I started to panic because of the separation. I felt like I was getting left behind. When I panic I start to get emotional. This bouldering part of the hike, where you had to scramble across the rocks, didn't feel like hiking anymore. The fear of falling and failing really crept in. I'm pretty sure I was most afraid of landing on my head and it cracking open like an egg. Just a scrambled pile of Abbie on the rocks. *Don't worry about me. I got this. Just casually dying over here in my negative self-talk.* My mind continued to focus on the worst-case scenario.

I remember seeing everybody else across and feeling rushed to get across on my own. I didn't like the pressure of people watching me, either. It all freaked me out.

They are judging me. That idiot over there is gonna crash. They are making fun of me for sure. I got consumed by what everybody was thinking about me.

I had forgotten to be more observant in what others were doing. I had gotten a few steps behind and started to panic a bit. Sarah called over to me to check in and I immediately started crying. Full tears, down my face. I felt like they were all leaving me behind. More thoughts welled up inside. *I can't do this. I am not going to make it. This elevation gain is too out of reach. I'm holding people up and falling behind. I will always be left behind.*

Being pushed to my limit, the other leader Scott came bounding back over toward me, taking my hand and guiding me over the rocks. I felt relieved and a bit embarrassed. He gave me a big smile and I made my way back over to the group. I took a few deep breaths, wiped my eyes, and put one foot in front of the other.

After another half mile, the trail flattened out. We rounded a corner and there sat Lower Reed Lake. Angels came down to sing as the sky opened up to a beautiful blue. The water was aquamarine, pristine and so calm. With an incredible view I looked back down at where we had just come from. Tears welled up in my eyes for the whole landscape was breathtakingly beautiful. I gave a shout-out prayer and a warm smile for I had made it, I did it. I was at the top of a mountain.

With a bit of wind in the air, our leaders instructed us to get our tents put together before the sunset. Hannah and I ended up getting a spot that felt like we were on a cliff.

Our tent was definitely sitting at an angle, allowing for my inflatable pad and sleeping bag to roll into hers. I practiced laying down and I slid right into Hannah due to it being really wonky in there. We laughed about how we were really going to get to know each other better tonight.

Meal time together was us enjoying those squishy hiker's meal pouches. There was also powdered lasagna—you just add hot water, shake and stir, and let sit for 15 minutes. Someone made a brownie mix and we passed it around for all to try. It was terrible but really fun nonetheless.

After dinner we retired to our tents. I rested my head down. I had this great sense of accomplishment wash over my body. Something that I didn't think I could do, I had pushed myself past the fear, past the *you will suck at this*, and made it to the final destination. My asthma was not affected on this hike at all.

During the hike, I had a dialogue with myself that I wanted to be really good at it. I wanted to be the best hiker. I didn't want to ask for help. I wanted to show everyone that I could do this really hard thing. Crying on that trail transported me and transformed my mind. I am capable of doing so much more than what my fear is holding me back from. My body and mind are conspiring together to cheer me on.

Hiking a mountain in Alaska became a significant marker of success for me. Not just physically, but mentally and emotionally. I learned that my body was more capable of doing things than I thought it was. Yes, I have asthma and yes, I do not have the greatest knees. But it wasn't a race to the top. I took my time and stopped as needed. I didn't get left behind. And I didn't hold anyone up. Afterall, there were a bunch of bad knees in the group and another asthmatic. We were all in it together.

Since the trip, I have found myself stepping into new opportunities with a "Hell Yes" mentality. No matter what challenge I might face, I have a new attitude toward the fears that used to hold me down. Fears that held me back and kept me small. I have made new pathways and connection points in my brain. Anything is possible.

So now in Oregon when friends ask me to go for a hike, I say yes without a doubt. I know I can do it. I just make sure I put those same Merrell hiking boots on that I wore in Alaska. Lacing them up, I feel empowered to go after the next adventure. Propelled forward, there are no more excuses, I just go.

ALL THINGS ARE POSSIBLE

CHECK IN ON YOURSELF

Think about three things that are holding you back from experiencing greatness—fears, past hurts, trials—and say those challenges aloud.

On this page write a message that reminds you of the strength you have within yourself.

CHAPTER 17

Cherry Blossoms on Salmon Street

Nature's pink confetti fills Salmon Street in Southeast Portland every spring. City planners many moons ago lined this street specifically with cherry blossom trees.

Every spring on these brown branches, as the temperature gets slightly warmer by the end of March, green buds start to pop out from the dormant winter. Then green leaves form, giving the trees voluminous form, depth, and texture. This unfolding of nature is very mysterious but I know it is basic photosynthesis. As another week or two passes, the trees start to develop small blossoms. Like a suprise party—POP!, overnight the street is pink. Each branch bows and bends over the sidewalks and into the street. Heavy from all the blossoms, these branches still carry a lightness as a small breeze blows through.

It's worth noting that Portland winters are gray. More gray than a Pantone color swatch. With a constant drizzle of rain for over six months, when spring arrives there is finally a break in the gray. Many trees and plants stay green year round here, but nothing feels as joyous as when these cherry blossoms let loose their expansive pink petals. The change of seasons, as they mysteriously arrive, brings the hope everything is connected to something bigger and something greater.

When spring unfolds her wings, the street that I live on brings forth new life, and I quickly forget the months of gray that preceded. The spring season is an important marker because that which was dead, doesn't have the final say. Spring reveals the workings of hidden goodness tucked away under ground. Daffodils and tulips come up first, giving signs that winter may be nearing her end. Birds return to their homes, more perennials stick out their budding heads, and people open their doors to prep their gardens. The cherry blossom trees are slow to open and reveal their pink colors. Each branch becomes more full of blossoms, showing off its voluptuous petals. The tree bends its branches and bows in the wind. The sun gives the street a complete makeover and every person who encounters such beauty just has to pause to take it all in. The bikers, the dog walkers, and the passersby all stop in their tracks in awe of this raw beauty unfolding before them. Pictures try to capture but only serve as a mini memory.

In the spring of 2020, another gray winter had finally passed. There was the physical reminder that my favorite trees always change color. The pink blossoms would return. Covid was something we were all learning about. A two-week shutdown in March became a year-plus shutdown. *Was I allowed to go outside and enjoy the beauty? Were we allowed to enjoy anything?* These blossoms were the only thing that gave me hope. With the trees turning color, it was a tangible expression that spring would come again.

Rainy season in Portland lasts from about October 'til late June. I might be exaggerating these gray sky days but in some ways, I'm not. Let me explain. When the rain hits late fall, there are breaks every now and again for sun rays, but most every Portlander is on a vitamin D supplement because we just don't have access to the sun. Living in the PNW is not for the faint of heart. Wind, rain, and not your typical downpour often scatter our days. As you step outside, this constant drizzle has your hair getting fuzzier than your best sweater. Putting a hat on, you don't even really know why you tried to style your hair.

Rain boots are a must and it's a constant fight between how many layers you should throw together. Then repeat and do it all over again the next day. For weeks, even months.

Winter in Portland rotates between shades of gray. It is almost like a romantic notion because it leaves people staying cozy inside amber lighting at bars, candles lit, blankets big, music that allows you to linger, and warmth from your furnace.

Everyone knows that you need to have a getaway during this time. Traveling to the desert or Joshua Tree, visiting some friends in Arizona, or taking a trip to Mexico can make a big difference. You have to get out of the gray. It is so important for mental health to have something to look forward to.

During the pandemic, when the world was not operating as it normally does, traveling out of the gray was nearly impossible. We were told to stay home and stay safe.

I found myself one afternoon going outside in March 2020, opening my door to a pink wonderland. Seeing the petals falling from the trees, I noticed how heaps of petals were mounding up, filling the ground, piling up over cars, and covering the sidewalks. It was this natural confetti, compostable pink dust, that no matter how hard you tried, this pinkness was going to get stuck all over you. The air was sweet like cotton candy as my allergies went wild.

Reaching down with my hands, I grabbed a big heap from the ground. Picking up these petals and placing them into the palm of my hand, I noticed some blossoms were fully intact. Gently, I let them bounce between my hands, back-and-forth between my fingertips.

Some fell between my feet, lightly cascading down and landing next to all the other petals.

I repeated this again, bending down and reaching into a pile of more blossoms. Everything was covered in pink—the whole street, all the way down as far as I could see. I grabbed as many as I could carry, stuffing them in my pockets. I was collecting them to let them dry in my apartment. The act of getting outside, scooping up what nature had to offer, and then presenting it back as a gift to myself gave me hope.

That time in my life made it really easy to fall into the depths of winter and even as the spring approached, the thoughts and fears, the worries and challenges still remained. Much of my stress came from the uncertainty of being a small business owner due to the pandemic. I didn't know how I was going to keep paying my bills. I worried about finding new work opportunities if all my events remained closed. I needed to figure out more work for myself and when I could safely visit my family again.

These petals were mine and yet they were everyone's all at the same time. Winter wasn't going to have its grip or final thought. The cherry blossoms give hope that winter doesn't last forever.

My small practice of collecting petals year after year after year has become a marker of hope. From a time that was so hard and difficult, when we were so isolated and alone, I felt connected to a bigger reality and expansive truth. My perspective shifted even as things came to pass and colors faded. Salmon Street was going to come alive again. Hope returned as hope remained.

BETTER
TO BE
IN AWE
THAN IN
DOUBT

CHECK IN ON YOURSELF

Grab some flower petals, basil leaves, etc... and hold them in your hands. Notice how they feel and what is brought up when you connect your skin to nature.

Use this page to draw out the petals or leaves you have found.

CHAPTER 18

Timothy Lake

I t was time for a road trip. I needed to get out of town to some water, which is always my ideal resting place. I filled up with gas, loaded up on snacks, a lawn chair, and some fun noodles. I had my swimsuit underneath my cut off overall shorts. My hair was wild with the windows down.

Before I peeled out of town to head east into the mountains, I made sure to take a pit stop at a local pastry cafe. Little T Baker is known for their seasonal danishes. It was peachy time, and this danish had some slices centered in cream cheese. The crunch when I bit down blew my mind every time. I slipped a bag inside my car and made my way, driving for just over an hour. I took US 26 to Oregon Sky Road, and cued the holy angel's chorus. Rounding the bend, I ended up at Timothy Lake in all her glory. Typically I camp here at Timothy Lake, but this time I just made a day trip.

There was an eagle flying overhead. It soared and swooped down to catch lunch in its mouth, then rose back up into the sky. The pine trees and I were impressed.

I reached the dock that extended out into the water at the main campsite. It is for all to use, mostly for people to put their boats in and out. The lake doesn't allow large motors so it was pretty calm waters. There was not going to be any Sea-Doo party, just many kayaks, canoes, and paddle boards. Lunging out of my car, I walked across some gravel and headed onto a dock of wooden planks. I slid my Birkenstock sandals off my feet. Walking to just about the end, there was a sign that said "no wading or sunbathing." I disregarded and slipped my feet into the water.

Time seemed to stop and the sun went higher in the sky. As I sat down on the edge of the dock the coolness of the water was a refreshing change from the heat in the city. The summer warmth and the vitamin D felt so good on my skin. I noticed a lot of fun, colorful floaties around. Some kids had a unicorn, other people had big air mattresses blown up underneath tarps, and some people barbecued and snacked on their chips. The air smelled of burgers with a splash of sunscreen. I made my way back to my car to grab my lawn chair. I slung it over my shoulder, along with my tote bag and my backpack. I had fun noodles under my right arm and a cooler with food in my left. I made my way through a path in the forest, dodging an occasional biker. Slapping a few mosquitoes here and there, I tried to find the spot. The spot where I was going to set up for the next few hours. It was crucial to be someplace where I would have some privacy, but where I would also be able to rest my body. It seemed to be a secret spot. A place that I didn't want anybody else to know.

I observed two little girls who started playing in the water together. They were maybe five years old and sang Frozen songs. One girl pranced around, dipped her hands into the water and splashed. The other giggled and carried about just the same. Two people paddled by on their stand-up paddle boards. One had a dog in a basket on the front, while the other had the cooler and the sunscreen in the backpack. There was a dad who used a kayak and pulled his kid behind in a blowup flamingo. They laughed and carried on. Others dipped in their kayaks and started to take off with top speed across the lake. I noticed a couple of sailboats moving quietly with the wind. I took out my Danish from the paper bag and it crinkled loudly. Laying it in my hand, I snapped a Polaroid picture as I held it to the sky hoping that the cream cheese and the peach juice wouldn't run down my arm. I quickly caught it and the stickiness across my arm tasted really sweet. I bit down and the crunch threw pastry chunks around me. My lap was now covered in powdered sugar. I brushed it off.

I pulled some daisies along the path and decided to hold them in my left hand as I drew them in my sketchbook, noticing the intricacies of every petal and how they were connected to the center. I took my watercolors and I painted, letting the water flow back and forth. I taught myself how to write with my left hand. It was a little wonky but it matched my drawing style so I kept it and on these pages, I was grateful to be found here.

Ready for a dip in the water, I started climbing over rocks, stepping over stones, seeing little fish swim at my feet. This was a special place. Refreshed was my soul.

There's something so good about enjoying life at a slower pace. With the week's routine, it always seemed so difficult to get out of town. Sometimes the drive was just too long, it's just not worth it. But every single time I find my spot, where I rest, open up my sketchbook, and start to draw, I notice that something changes inside of me. I slow down and I am able to notice what's around me. With all the clamor and noise happening, my view becomes a type of movie that's playing out.

When I have the chance to get out of the city, the noise, and the hustle, I get an opportunity to recharge. Because I am an entrepreneur, there is an overwhelming amount of pressure I put on myself to succeed, excel, and produce in every aspect of my day-to-day world.

Being in survival mode is tiring, so taking a break from normal routines helps clear my mind. I am able to refocus on what really matters to me. This is not an escape but a chance to explore and be found in a state of wonder. I reset, expanding my ability to be creative and create. I love connecting back to nature, and the simplicity found in just existing.

REST, RELEASE, REPEAT

CHECK IN ON YOURSELF

List out places and times when you feel at peace.

_____

_____

_____

_____

_____

_____

_____

_____

_____

_____

_____

_____

_____

_____

Reflect on how you are able to find rest in these moments.

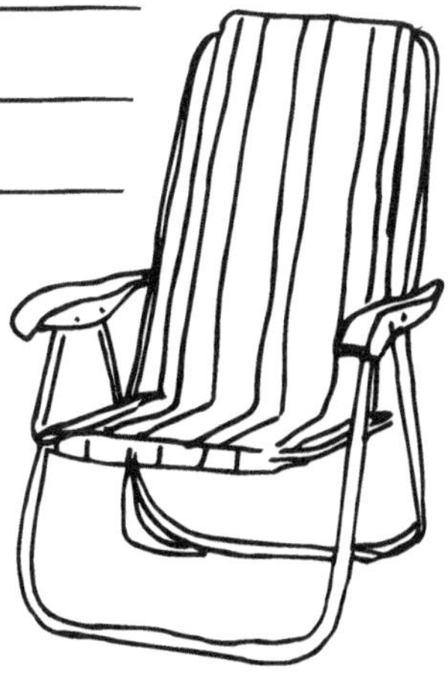

_____

_____

_____

_____

_____

_____

_____

_____

_____

_____

_____

_____

_____

_____

_____

_____

_____

_____

washing hands
washing pans
keep going

CHAPTER 19

Go Get 'Em Martha

Mary and Martha are two women who heard that a wise teacher was coming into town and would be visiting their house. The visit was not planned weeks in advance, but last minute, by word of mouth. While Martha took care of the logistics for their guest's arrival, Mary waited, watched, and sat. When Jesus arrived, Mary rested at Jesus' side, taking in all that he had to say. Martha got frustrated because Mary didn't give a helping hand to all that needed to be done.

This story is subversive in that women were not allowed to learn and listen to men teach. Jesus was subversive in the way he wanted to gather around these women. I see this story in two ways: often, women need to have a place to rest, and in the same thread, are to be very productive. Both are important. When we are on the move, it is not a bad thing, and yet there is importance in honing in on some healthy boundaries with how we spend our time and energy. We need to be present for our own needs, allowing time for rest, which ultimately helps us be refilled. There is space for accomplishing tasks that need to get done, but not at the expense of connecting back to ourselves or with others.

Teachers of this Biblical story often compare the two women, encouraging people to be honest if they are a "Martha" or a "Mary."

"Marthas" are the ones who put the show together, get that meal on the table, and make sure everyone is taken care of. They have the ability to work, organize and put momentum forward in what is needed. Marthas are about the details. Each one of us can be a Martha, multitasking and prioritizing getting the work done.

Marthas are bold, take charge, and push back with questions, having the courage to go into the unknown. It would be easy to misconstrue that Mary, on the other hand, was lazy, not wanting to be helpful, and not interested in being there for her sister to prepare for a guest.

I don't think Mary was lazy. Seizing moments to be fully present with others gives you opportunities to gain a great perspective on what really matters.

I think Mary allowed herself to be present with the guest who didn't get an official invite, who was just randomly in town popping by for a visit. The women did hear of his coming, yet they still didn't have much time to prepare for his arrival. News spread and Jesus would just show up when he was able to get there. With little notice, Mary positioned herself to take every moment in and treasure it.

Unlike "Marthas," "Marys" are the ones who are concerned with embracing others before themselves, captivated in the present moment to listen, learn, and be impacted. They have the ability to slow down, stay attentive to others' needs, and serve.

Marys are thoughtful, considerate, and have a heart to extend love to others through being present, while Marthas show their love through action and tunnel vision, but almost to a fault.

I talked to my friend Kristin about how we are "Marthas"— we have the "Girl Boss" or "Boss Lady" mentality, the hustle and the pressure to be doing all the things. There is a lot stacked up for women and placed on our shoulders to manage, navigate, and pursue. Societal expectations get positioned around us, especially when you're an entrepreneur.

Marthas get a bad rap for the work that they can accomplish and

get done. This stems from the Biblical story, and how much of church culture yells out, "Don't be a Martha," as if to say, "Don't concern yourself with being busy and don't go after your desires—put being present with others first." So many times it is seen as selfish to put yourself first and get work done for yourself. We are told to just wait, be patient, and be of service. This is a central theme to living a life of faith, but when taken out of context can be completely detrimental.

What I want you to know is that I think being a Martha is a good thing. It means that you can go after all the biggest desires and dreams in one moment and then the next, do the practical tasks that need to get done in your everyday life. My friend Kristin is a mom of two who is trying to bounce between taking care of her kids, pursuing her design career, fulfilling other family obligations, prioritizing her relationship with her husband, staying connected to friends, and wanting to plant as many vegetables in her garden as she can. From small to large tasks, no matter the emotional weight or physical stresses, she gets up every day and chooses to keep showing up in all the things. To recharge, she goes for a long drive and brings a book to read and a journal to write in. She knows that in order to keep afloat she needs times of rest. She is a Martha but has found moments to be a Mary—to sit and rest and recharge.

It is an admirable thing to be a Martha. I like to say, "Go Get Em' Martha!" to my friend Kristin. This phrase has become an encouraging line that we use towards each other when there is something big we are tackling. There is power in saying this because it amplifies the "you can do it" charge, that no matter what nothing is impossible. Marthas prove that we *can* do it all. At the same time, we need to find our Mary moments. May you have the understanding and confidence in yourself to take a step back from time to time, giving yourself a break. May you REST and be present for your needs, as well as the needs of those around you. May your inner Martha and Mary sing in harmony, taking turns with the melody.

GO
GET 'EM
MARTHA

CHECK IN ON YOURSELF

Write and reflect out ways you can honor the Mary and Martha in yourself and in others.

_____

_____

_____

_____

_____

_____

_____

_____

_____

_____

_____

_____

_____

_____

_____

_____

_____

CHAPTER 20

Pura Vida in Costa Rica

I had never been to Costa Rica before. I had signed myself up for another Ivy Brand trip, and specifically a M.A.D. (Make A Difference) trip. This type of trip was very special to the DNA of Ivy. We weren't just going on epic adventures; we would be making a difference doing some humanitarian work at a local non-profit organization. The trip was pitched as nine days full of fun and a lot of hard work. I was ready to travel internationally and make a new group of friends in this tropical landscape.

Upon arriving in Costa Rica, we spent a few days getting to know one another while traveling around in a fifteen-passenger van. We bounced between exploring waterfalls, hot springs, and whitewater rafting. Good conversations, good food, and so many good laughs. Then it was time to journey towards Lake Arenal, the site of the local non-profit organization. Our next five days would be spent digging a foundation for a building that was in progress of being built. Wheelbarrow after wheelbarrow, shovel to hard ground, we dug up the red earth. The work was tough, but with everyone pitching in we successfully completed the part of the project we came to do. Two full days in the hot sun. Lunch breaks, water breaks, and sweat breaks. I felt a deep sense of pride. On the third day, we had options to work on other parts of the property, so I decided to venture off and complete a different project.

Six of us crammed into a small vehicle and drove down a road called "oh shit road." It is not really an actual road, but more like a bumpy, steep, grassy path. We endured ten minutes of winding through foliage, maneuvering over rocks, and dodging various trees until we made it to our spot. The goal here was to move rocks around in a lightly flowing stream, to dam up an area making a small pool for people to sit in. After jumping out of the car, four of us made our way downriver while two stayed closer to the car.

I quickly realized I wished I would have worn my swimsuit. I had on regular shorts and a T-shirt and wasn't prepared to get soaked. Everyone started to pitch in and work together to move rocks around. We were in the water, which was up to about our hips, looking for rocks to position in a semicircle. The water was cool and felt good from the warm air. Looking down in the water I could easily see different dark spots. Reaching down, I was able to detect a rock and would gently feel around the sides to learn the size. If I could move it on my own I did, or other times I would ask for a friend to come help.

Our leader, Steve, gave guidance and direction for the vision of this swimming hole project. If we were in fact to semi-dam a part of the current, we needed to build up a wall across one side. There seemed to be a natural wall already started, so we were going to use that as a base. I found a rock and would pass it off to my friend Chelsea to place it where it needed to go. We did this rearranging and carrying of rocks for over an hour. Diving my hands down, the water became murky from dirt being kicked up as I pulled the stones out. The ground was not easy to walk on and we were frequently being tripped up.

There was a quiet joy surfacing as I did this work, knowing that girls would be using this area to relax after a long hot day on the property. The land and grounds were being built up as a place for girls coming out of abusive living conditions and sex trafficking. All of those kids calling this place home were going to find a calm resting spot along this gentle stream.

I will say that I got into a competitive mindset while working on this task. I was determined to move just about any rock that I put my hands on, which honestly was impossible at times. I frequently had to call Steve over to actually move said rock that I had found. Or if it was more boulder-sized, we would roll it together into the spot we wanted it. Back and forth we'd go, building up this wall and daming this stream to create the pool.

Completely wet, with my hair stuck to my shoulders, squatting down into the water I felt two rocks piled on top of one another. I knew I couldn't move these, but I figured if I could get help moving the top one, then the other would come free. Steve was right there, using all of his strength and he couldn't get either rock to budge. I did the next best thing, I started digging around the sides of the rocks, moving and scrapping smaller ones at the base. This proved to work because we got the large boulder to move. IT MOVED. WE FELT IT WIGGLE. There was an excitement that burst out and huge smiles were on our faces. *Could it be that we were going to be able to move these rocks? If we could clear the base, it would be easier for people to walk around in.*

Steve started to lean and roll this massive rock to the right. I didn't want my feet to get in the way so I moved my body to the left. I took a couple more steps over to the left, Steve continued to roll the rock and OUT OF NOWHERE my left pinkie finger got smashed between a rock and a hard place. I honestly don't even know how exactly it happened. So quick and without warning. Initially it just felt like a small thing. The rock had landed on my finger and it stung a little. "Ouch that hurt," I said.

"Was that your finger?"

"Yeah, it's okay, I am okay."

"I am so sorry I didn't know your finger was there."

I shook my left hand out, in total shock, not truly understanding what just had happened. I jolted my whole hand in the water and brought it up to look at.

"Are you okay?" he asked.

"Look at how cool that is," I said, showing him my finger that was freshly cut.

The look on his face was not a pleasant one and he said, "No that is not cool. Let's get you some bandages."

I shoved my hand back in the water, because blood was now flowing freely. As I pulled my hand up, immediately the guts of my pinkie finger were no longer on the inside; they were on the outside.

As we took the lovely, bumpy "oh shit road" back up to the

top of the property, I needed to get some medical attention at the main building. My new friend Lucy was a nurse and used her T-shirt to wrap my finger and we all crammed back into that car. One of the girls threw her arm around me. I was in a bit of pain, but feelings of gratitude overwhelmed me more. I knew my finger was going to be okay and that I was being taken care of. A sense of comfort overwhelmed me knowing that I was with a professional nurse and close friends.

Immediately the team located the first aid kit, as Lucy mentioned we needed to get the bleeding to stop. Looking at my pinkie finger she kept telling me she thought I would need stitches. Y'all, I have never needed stitches before—never in my life have I ever broken a bone. The only kind of medical surgery I had was getting my wisdom teeth out, but they put you under for that so I don't even know what happened.

I didn't freak out about hearing I needed stitches. I trusted I was in good hands and had an overarching peace that things would work out. I wasn't blindly putting my trust out there, but asked questions on what the next steps were to take, how we would get to the best clinic, and receive the stitches I needed to get my finger healing.

Accidents happen all the time. And often they happen when we least expect it. In this situation, I learned that I could remain calm, and in doing so, stay in a good headspace. I didn't bring on any extra anxiety or worry. I stayed focused on getting the medical care I needed.

In any other situation, I would have been racing in worries causing me to cry. I would have been overwhelmed to the point of panic, thus making the pain worse. Fear would have been the focal point and would have driven me towards anxiety and thinking of worst-case scenarios. I didn't know how to stop those trains of thoughts when they started. Wrapped up in an emotional response, I wouldn't have been able to think or respond clearly. I never wanted to inconvenience anyone or be a focal point of attention for getting hurt.

But this day, the complete opposite happened from all other previous experiences. I dialed in a breathing technique, inhaling and exhaling to keep my system calm. Instead of running with negative thoughts, I told myself positive phrases. Everything was going to be okay and I didn't need to worry. Instead of overthinking, I turned to others for comfort. I knew and believed I was in good hands. People were there to take care of me; I was not alone. I didn't have to figure anything out by myself. While in shock, I was still able to hold this sense of peace in my body. This all comes from a greater knowing, a faith that I could trust those around me because they were for me. I leaned into my new friends and I was met with compassion, provision, and strength. They remained calm with me.

The whole experience could have been really traumatic, and I typically would have turned to my previous methods to cope with the pain. But here I was calm, even laughing at times, feeling a covering over me that I was going to be okay—a reflection of both my growth, and being surrounded by others who took care of me. I had Steve who immediately recognized I needed help, Emelia comforting me on the bumpy ride, nurse Lucy who bandaged me up, Sarah who didn't leave my side, and finally, the organization founder to speak Spanish at the clinic and translate for me.

I was on a trip of a lifetime and I knew I couldn't let some stitches stop me from enjoying the rest of my day or my time in Costa Rica. Upon returning back to our condos, six shots to numb my finger and eight stitches later, I was able to get changed and return to the others for the night's activities. We were taking salsa and bachata dance lessons. Thankfully I didn't need a functional pinky finger to dance. Later on, I learned that Steve thought my finger was gone, busted up completely. As I type this, I still don't have a fully functioning pinkie finger. The tendon is intact, I just don't have complete use of it back yet. As with any journey toward healing, time will be on my side. And if I am lucky, the next dance lesson I take will be just as fun as that one. All ya gotta do is pop those hips.

DEEP BREATHS AND THANKFULNESS

CHECK IN ON YOURSELF

Reflect on a time in your life when you were in between a rock and hard place. List the ways you were able to breathe through those experiences or lean on your community.

_____

_____

_____

_____

_____

_____

_____

_____

_____

_____

_____

_____

_____

_____

_____

_____

BE INSPIRED

LOOK
UP

Resources

This is a go-to resource section to find my favorite snacks, movement for your body, breathwork exercises, and Pep Talks! Flip through anytime. Be encouraged and dig in. You are amazing. ☺

Go-To Snacks

1. **Cheese Stick + Apple + Nuts.** Feel like a kid again with mozzarella string cheese. Slice up a favorite apple and add a handful of nuts.

2. **English Muffin with Peanut Butter + Raspberries on top.** Toast your muffins and spread the peanut butter. Load up the berries on top.

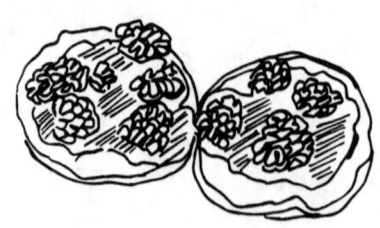

3. Wheat Thins Crackers + Carrots + Hummus.
Buy some rainbow variety of carrots
to add some color. Slice up a big
handful and serve with your
favorite hummus. Add in 2
handfuls of crackers for a
crunch.

4. Plain Greek Yogurt + Granola + Jam or Seasonal Fruit.
Scoop 3-4 tablespoons of yogurt in a bowl. Pour in a
half cup of granola. Toss in your favorite berries or jam.
Stir and enjoy.

5. **Popcorn + Pretzel Chips + 4 Dark Chocolate Squares.**
   Add 4 handfuls of popcorn with 2 handfuls of pretzels.
   Break up the chocolate and mix together. Great grab-
   and-go snack.

6. **Favorite Smoothie Recipe with the Clementines.**
   See page 207 for full recipe.

7. **Matcha + Biscotti.** Matcha recipe—with cardamom, honey, Milkadamia, Mizuba. A great combo and perfect for dunking! See page 208 for full recipe.

8. **Sardines in Olive Oil on Whole Wheat Crackers + Cream Cheese + Roasted Red Peppers + Arugula.** Smear cream cheese on crackers and pile high ingredients as desired. Drizzle extra oil over top.

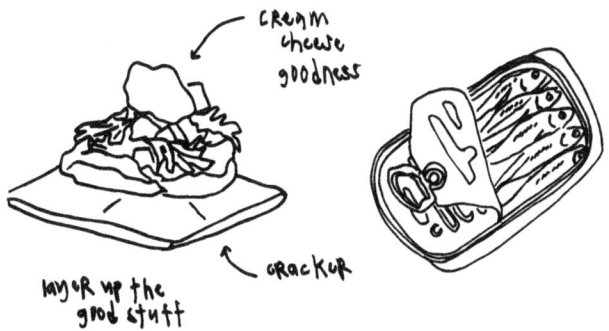

cream cheese goodness

crackur

layer up the good stuff

9. Huge glass of Coconut Water + Pear.
(But any fruit is good.)

10. Avocado, Bacon, Egg Toast + True Tea. (My favorite is the Renew blend.) Cook egg as you prefer. Slice an avocado on toasted bread with fried bacon. Drizzle honey over top for a little added bonus.

Smoothie Recipe

2 clementines

1 banana

2 crushed ginger cubes (from Target freezer section)

handful of spinach

½ cup of Greek yogurt

¼ cup of Milkadamia

4-5 cubes of ice

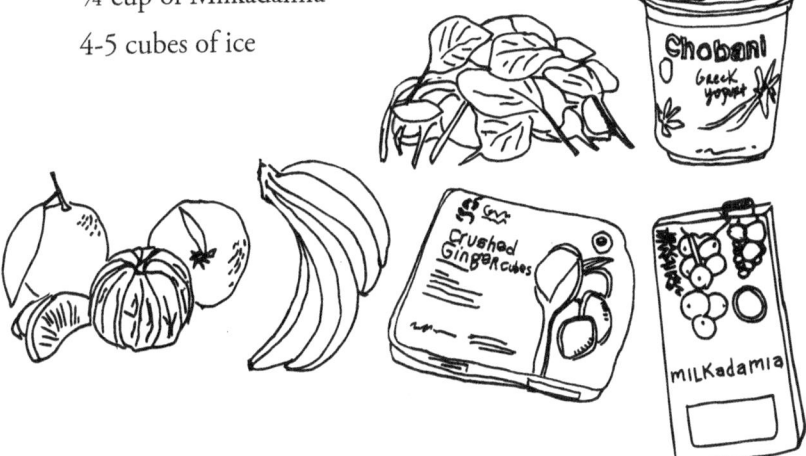

Place all ingredients into a blender and mix
on high until everything is smooth. Pour in a tall
glass and add a straw if you want! Slurp and sip away.

Mizuba Matcha Tea Latte Recipe

Heat 8 oz of milk on low or use a frother (I like Milkadamia, the original flavor.)

Place 4 oz medium heat water + 1 teaspoon matcha in mason jar (My favorite brand is Mizuba.)

Shake for 3 minutes

¼ teaspoon ground nutmeg

Sprinkle of cardamom

Stir matcha, milk, and spices together

Add honey to taste

Enjoy!

Movement

All of these are fun things that I try to do on a regular basis to help ease my body and mind.

Stretches and Activation for your body

1. Arms in the Doorway

   Press your forearm at a 90 degree angle against a door frame. Lean forward and then switch to the other arm.

2. Rotation with Stretched Arms

   In table top position, drop one arm and thread it through. Reaching to the opposite side, rotate your shoulder towards the ground.

3. Dancing in Living Room

Let the music rip and let your hair fly.

4. Plank

Get down on the ground with forearms and toes, holding your core with a flat back.

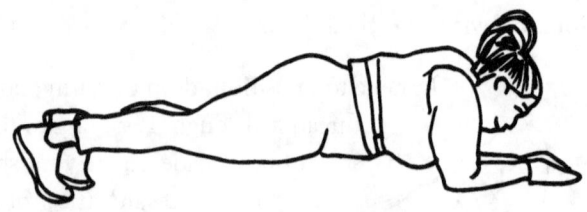

5. Neck Roll

Gently rotate your
neck in circles,
moving from clock-
wise to counter
clockwise.

6. Sumo Squat

Bend both knees, placing
your feet shoulder-width apart.

7. Walking Outside

The fresh air will feel good on your skin.

8. Starfish Stretch

Lay out flat on the ground, reaching your limbs as far as you can out from your body.

Breathwork

5 exercises and practices to help calm your anxious thoughts and slow down your nervous system.

1. Hold hands on heart
   Close your eyes or keep them open
   Think of a positive message or phrase
   Or
   Bring to mind something you are grateful for
   Or
   A good thing that has happened recently
   Breathe in and out normally for 2-5 minutes

2. For two counts inhale through your nose, then for two counts exhale out your mouth

During this time, think of a phrase you can break into two parts.

The first half of the phrase say in your mind during the inhale.

The second half of the phrase say in your mind during the exhale.

Repeat this 5-10 times in a row.

Example Phrase: "I am enough today."

Inhale in "I am," then exhale out "enough today."

3. Lay on the ground with both hands on your stomach. Start to breathe through your nose, deep from within your diaphragm. Exhale through your mouth. Keeping your shoulders on the ground, notice how your chest rises and falls with each breath.

   Position yourself in this spot for 5 minutes.

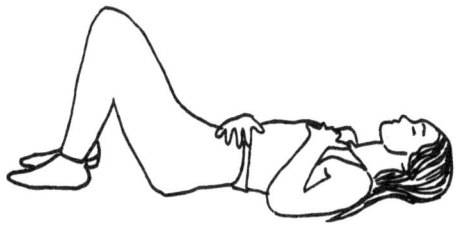

4. Extend your hands toward the sky. As you reach your arms up, breathe in. Let your hands fall to heart center and exhale through this stretch.

5. Timed breath in and out. Inhale on the odd numbers and exhale on the even numbers. Take your time counting, allowing at least a second per number. Focus on the number and close your eyes.

Pep Talks

This section is for a quick fix for those times you need it most. Be encouraged! I am here cheering you on.

Pep Talks

1. Relax your jaw.
2. Spread some kindness.
3. Breathe. Inhale and exhale.
4. One thing at a time.
5. Get outside.
6. Take a break.
7. You are not alone.
8. Write a letter.
9. Move your body, work it out.
10. Freakin rest already.

PEP TALK #1

RELAX YOUR JAW

Remember to smile.
Check in on yourself throughout the day.

PEP TALK #2

SPREAD SOME KINDNESS

Embrace the one vessel you've got.
When you are able, fill others up.

PEP TALK #3

BREATHE

Take a moment for yourself.

PEP TALK #4

ONE THING AT A TIME

But seriously, each day has enough trouble of its own.
There is only so much you can control.

PEP TALK #5

GET OUTSIDE

Fresh air and looking up at the moon can change your perspective. Be found in a place of wonder as your feet hit some pavement or dirt road. Notice your surroundings.

PEP TALK #6

Let yourself have a pause. Think one amazing positive thought about yourself. Repeat!

PEP TALK #7

YOU ARE NOT ALONE

Out at sea or standing on concrete, lean into your community.
A friend or loved one is only a phone call away.
Find connection even in the stars. You belong here.

PEP TALK #8

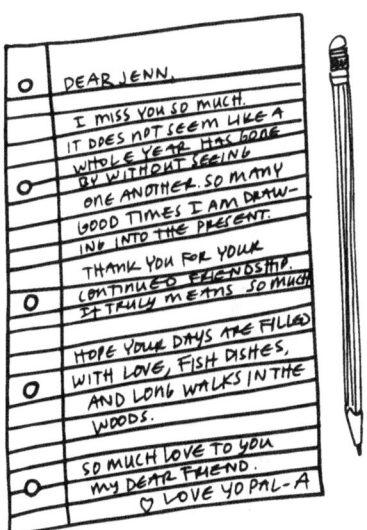

Snail mail is fun to send.
Encourage a friend or loved one.

PEP TALK #9

MOVE YOUR BODY, WORK IT OUT

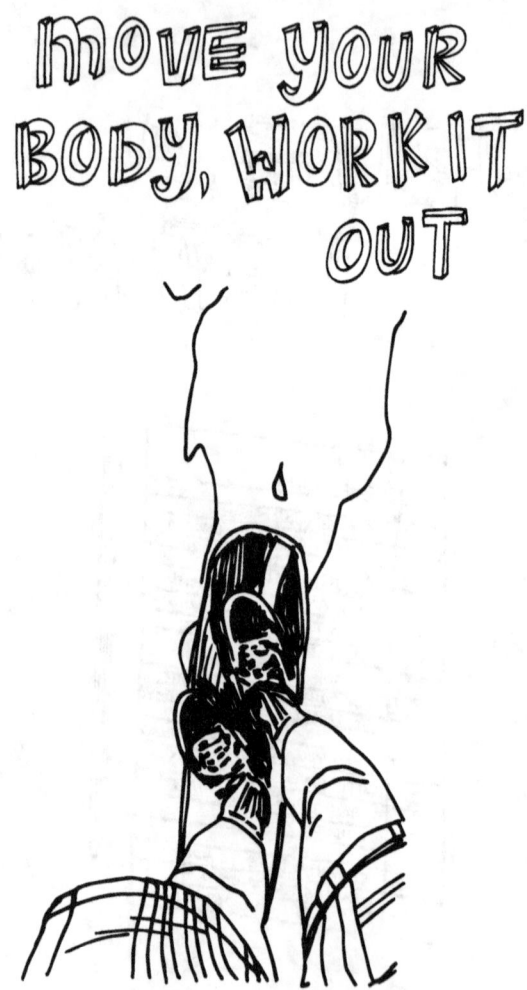

Feeling stuck or overwhelmed, just get your body moving. Have you stretched today? Danced in your pajamas? Take 5, 10, or 30 minutes to just be.

PEP TALK #10

FREAKIN REST ALREADY

The world needs you to stay true and strong in your vision and gifts. Get some rest and then get back to it. And not just Netflix or mindless scrolling.

THANK YOU

Acknowledgements

I really want to say thank you with all of my guts to:

Joy at Punchline Publishers for giving me an avenue to pursue self-publishing. This dream project would have been tabled if we hadn't jumped on that Zoom call. I am forever grateful for you and believing in my work.

Amelia for all your edits. Working with you has been such a gift. I would have given up a thousand times, but grateful you kept the comments coming along with the encouragement.

Jessica for putting your eye on every sentence. I appreciate you so much and your attention to detail. Thank you for cheering me on and answering my Instagram post.

Bonnie to you I owe so much gratitude. Thank you for showing up and coming alongside me. I feel more comfortable in my body through your presence, friendship, and mentorship.

Chelsea for being a queen graphic designer, helping get my scattered ideas to a complete beautiful visual. I love that we met in Costa Rica and I am continually grateful to be adventuring with you.

Janelle for putting all the pages together and making everything look so GOOD. You are amazing and I feel so fortunate to have you on this project.

Gabbie for your hand in crafting those early drafts and reminding me that these stories were worth sharing. This book has breath because you believed in my work many years ago.

Kelsey for all your formatting wizardry in helping me get organized and making me look professional in those early stages. You are a remarkable human.

Allie for always being my buddy-oh-pal. You have been my biggest cheerleader in life and my best friend. I hope this book can be an encouragement to your kids.

About the Author

Abigail Renola Tjaden is an illustrator, designer, professor, and entrepreneur. Originally from Minnesota, she has been calling Portland, Oregon home for the past eleven years. Abigail has her MFA and BFA in fine arts, as well as a BS degree in secondary education. She is an adjunct professor at Portland State University, teaching digital tools and silkscreening in the Graphic Design department. Recently, she was a finalist for an award in Women in Excellence and Creative Entrepreneurship at Elevate, a women's conference.

In 2013, after a transformative trip to Tunisia, North Africa, Abigail started her own business: ARTJADEN. Back in Portland, at a house called Fort Awesome, she began hand-printing apparel and illustrating greeting cards. She has since collaborated and illustrated for numerous brands, a featured artist in markets coast to coast. Her work can be found in local shops around the country.

Abigail's notable experiences include painting a mural at a nonprofit in Costa Rica, being juried into two international art residency programs, one called HANGAR in Lisbon, Portugal, and another called SÍM in Reykjavík, Iceland, exhibiting twice at The National Stationery Show in New York City, and creating visual journaling sessions for Instrument, a Portland-New York business creative agency. You can stay connected on Instagram at @artjadendesigns and visit www.artjaden.com.

NOTES WRITE SKETCH

Fill these last pages up! It is all you! Have some fun!

www.ingramcontent.com/pod-product-compliance
Lightning Source LLC
Chambersburg PA
CBHW061147120626
46546CB00005B/1962

*9 7 8 1 9 5 5 0 5 1 2 2 4 *